What is Palestine-Israel?

What is Palestine-Israel?
Answers to Common Questions

Commissioned by Mennonite Central Committee

Sonia K. Weaver

Herald Press
Scottdale, Pennsylvania
Waterloo, Ontario

Acknowledgments

The author would like to thank Deborah Fast, Alain Epp Weaver, Jan Janzen, Rick Janzen, J. Daryl Byler, William Janzen, Mark Beach, Patricia Shelly, Calvin Shenk, Marie Shenk, John F. Lapp, Ron Flaming, Levi Miller, Tim Seidel, and Chris Hoover Seidel for having read through previous versions of this booklet. Their perceptive comments have greatly strengthened this piece.

Library of Congress Cataloging-in-Publication Data
Weaver, Sonia K.
    What is Palestine-Israel? : answers to common questions / Sonia K. Weaver;
    commissioned by Mennonite Central Committee.
        p. cm.
    Includes bibliographical references.
    ISBN 978-0-8361-9366-4 (pbk. : alk. paper)
    1. Palestine in Christianity—Miscellanea. 2. Israel (Christian theology)—Miscellanea.
    3. Church work—Palestine—Miscellanea. 4. Church work—Mennonites—Miscellanea.
    I. Mennonite Central Committee. II. Title.
    BT93.8.W43 2007
    956.9405—dc22   2006101779

WHAT IS PALESTINE-ISRAEL?
Copyright © 2007 by Herald Press,
Scottdale, Pa. 15683
    Published simultaneously in Canada by Herald Press, Waterloo, Ont. N2L 6H7.
    All rights reserved.
International Standard Book Number: 978-0-8361-9366-4
Printed in United States of America
Design by Roberta Fast
Photos by Matthew Lester and Ryan Beiler
Photos on pages 30 and 40 by Richard Lord

14 13 12 11 10 09 08 07   10 9 8 7 6 5 4 3 2 1

To order or request information, please call
1-800-759-4447 (individuals);
1-800-245-7894 (trade).
Web site: www.heraldpress.com

Palestinian children flying kites at Damascus Gate, Old City.

Jibril and sister Ana am in outside their home in Palestine. Bullets have hit the walls of their home.

Table of Contents

4. Religion

5. Continuing Conflict, Sources of Hope

6. How Mennonites are Responding, How You Can Help

7. Resources for Further Study

A boy holds a piece of art work showing the daily violence in the Gaza Strip at the Shoroq wa Amal (sunrise and hope) children's center in Khan Younis, Gaza Strip.

Introduction

1. Introduction

The combined name Palestine-Israel only hints at the deep fissures dividing this land. An introductory booklet like this one can only offer a brief glimpse of such a complex conflict. Mennonites in Canada and the United States regularly ask Mennonite workers in Palestine-Israel about the complexities of the Palestinian-Israeli conflict. This book presents some of the questions Mennonite workers in Palestine regularly receive from supporters in Canada, the United States, and beyond, along with straightforward answers. While the book grew out of the experience of Mennonite Central Committee (MCC), a relief, development, and peacebuilding agency of Mennonite and Brethren in Christ churches in Canada and the United States, it also pays attention to the work of other Mennonite mission and peacebuilding agencies in the country.

This booklet is organized by theme, but all of the areas are inter-related. You may jump in and out of the text according to your interest. Please remember that what you are reading is a necessarily simplified treatment of a complicated situation. For those wishing to learn more about Palestine-Israel, the final section includes resources for further information.

A street sign in Bethlehem that was run over by a tank during October 2001 fighting.

Geography

2. Geography

To discuss geography in the Middle East is no simple matter. Even seemingly straightforward questions like "Where do you live?" or "Where are you from?" can have major political implications for Palestinians, Israelis, and internationals alike. What Palestinians and the international community call the Occupied Territories, for example, Israel calls Judea and Samaria or the "administered territories." The following section addresses the multiple meanings behind some of the most common geographical references.

What is Israel?

Israel is the name of the country claiming sovereign control over 78 percent of Mandate Palestine. Israel includes the Negev (Naqab in Arabic) Desert in the south, West Jerusalem and the coastal plains in the center, and the Galilee in the north. This area is also referred to as "Israel proper." Israel has annexed East Jerusalem and the Golan Heights, territories it occupied in 1967, but the international community has not recognized these annexations. Although Israel occupies the West Bank militarily, it has not annexed these territories, not wishing to absorb the Palestinians in these places as Israeli citizens.

Approximately seven million people live in the state of Israel. Israel's population is about 80 percent Jewish, 17 percent Muslim, and three percent Christian. Israel is a unique country because it defines itself as the state of all Jewish people throughout the world, rather than as a state of all of its citizens. As a result, Jewish citizens of Israel receive preferential treatment in all major aspects of social and political life, including schooling, healthcare, housing, and land use. Israel refers to its Arab citizens, who make up one-fifth of the country's population, as "Israeli Arabs." In recent years, however, these Arab citizens of Israel have increasingly begun to refer to themselves as "Palestinian citizens of Israel."

What is Palestine?

The name Palestine means different things to different people in different contexts. Sometimes Palestine refers to all of Mandate Palestine, which includes all the land between the Jordan River and the Mediterranean Sea. Great Britain administered this territory during the first part of the twentieth century through a mandate it received from the League of Nations, hence the name. Today Mandate Palestine includes Israel proper, the West Bank, and the Gaza Strip. The term Historical Palestine is also used to refer to approximately the same territory.

Palestine can also be used to designate only the West Bank (including East Jerusalem) and the Gaza Strip. This combination of territories would constitute the

Milade Thalgieh leaving the Church of the Nativity in Bethlehem.

State of Palestine in the event that a future independent Palestinian state was established. Many Palestinians hope for the creation of such a state as part of a final resolution to the Israel-Palestine conflict.

Why do some people refer to Palestine-Israel or Israel-Palestine?

These rather clumsy, interchangeable names represent attempts to refer to the land in question in a way that honors both Israeli and Palestinian attachment to the land. Saying Israel-Palestine or Palestine-Israel emphasizes that two peoples live in one land treasured by each as a homeland. Israel-Palestine and Palestine-Israel designate all of Mandate Palestine, including the West Bank, the Gaza Strip, and Israel

The shadow of Saliba Baddoun of Wi'am (The Palestinian Conflict Resolution Center) as he surveys the damage in the West Bank village of Beit Jala after the Israeli occupation of October 2001. An overturned Palestinian bulldozer lies in the background.

proper. Use of these names acknowledges that both Palestinians and Israelis claim the land and deserve to live there peacefully and securely.

What are the Occupied Territories?

In the context of the Palestinian-Israeli conflict, the term "Occupied Territories" refers to East Jerusalem, the West Bank, and the Gaza Strip. Together these territories constitute 22 percent of Historical Palestine. In the broader Middle Eastern context, "Occupied Territories" also includes the Golan Heights—Syrian territory occupied by Israel since 1967. The State of Israel does not consider East Jerusalem, the West Bank, and the Gaza Strip to be Occupied Territories. Instead, Israel annexed East Jerusalem into the state, and views the West Bank and the Gaza Strip as "administered" or "disputed" territories, rather than

as Occupied Territories. Some Israelis also refer to the West Bank by the biblical names of Judea and Samaria. Israeli settlers routinely call the Occupied Territories YESHA, an acronym of the Hebrew words for Judea, Samaria, and Gaza.

When Israel withdrew its settlers and soldiers from inside the Gaza Strip, it declared that the occupation of Gaza was finished. This declaration was puzzling because Israel had always insisted that Gaza, like the West Bank, was simply "administered" or "disputed," not occupied. Given the fact that Israel maintains full control over all of the Gaza Strip's borders with the outside world, most specialists in international law continue to consider the Gaza Strip to be occupied territory.

What is the West Bank?

The West Bank is a kidney-bean shaped territory, 5,860 kilometers square, extending from the city of

Jenin in the north to the city of Hebron in the south, with the Jordan River as its eastern edge. More than 2.5 million Palestinians live in the West Bank (including 250,000 in East Jerusalem), together with 430,000 Israeli settlers (190,000 of whom live in East Jerusalem settlements). Historically, East Jerusalem has been an integral part of the West Bank. Israel's construction of settlements, a network of settlement roads, and the separation barrier have all contributed to West Bank cities being separated from one another and to East Jerusalem being separated from the rest of the West Bank.

What is the Gaza Strip?

The Gaza Strip is a small sliver of land, 360 kilometers square, which hugs the Mediterranean Sea and the Egyptian border. Some 1.4 million Palestinians live in the Gaza Strip, two-thirds of whom are refugees. Half of the refugees live in Gaza's eight refugee camps. Overcrowding in Gaza's refugee camps is a major problem, with the population density in some camps reaching four to eight people per room. Since Israeli "disengagement" from the Gaza Strip in the summer of 1994, no Israeli settlers have lived in the Strip. Although the Israeli military withdrew from the heart of the Gaza Strip in 2004, it maintains full control over Gaza's borders with the rest of the world, making it

the world's largest open-air prison. Under international law the Gaza Strip therefore remains occupied territory.

Gazans enjoy few economic opportunities. In the past, most income generated by Gazans was earned by Palestinians working as day laborers in Israel, where they were considered a source of cheap labor. Harvard economist Sara Roy has analyzed how Israeli military regulations actively discouraged economic development in the Gaza Strip, a policy that Roy called "de-development." Beginning with the Oslo Accords in 1993, however, Israel began severely restricting the number of Gazans allowed into Israel to work. At the same time, Israel began importing workers from Asia and Eastern Europe as new sources of cheap labor. Today, the vast majority of Palestinians are rarely allowed to leave Gaza, be it to work in Israel or to travel to Jerusalem, the West Bank, or Egypt.

How are Israeli settlements altering the geography of Palestine-Israel?

The map on page 8 graphically demonstrates how Israeli settlements in the West Bank are turning Palestinian towns and villages into isolated islands or reservations. Israeli settlements, also known as colonies, have been strategically placed to create "facts on the ground" that fulfill Israel's political goals of claiming more territory.

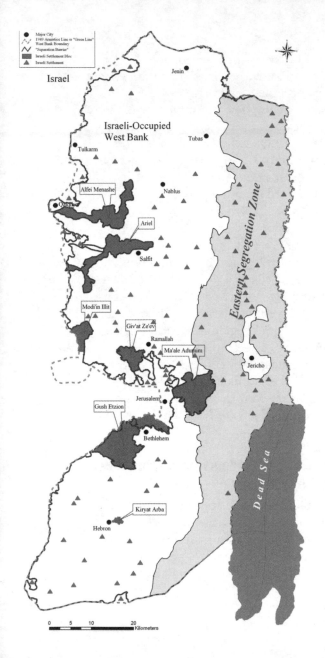

Legend:
- Major City
- 1949 Armistice Line or "Green Line" West Bank Boundary
- "Separation Barrier"
- Israeli Settlement Bloc
- Israeli Settlement

Israel

Israeli-Occupied West Bank

Jenin

Tulkarm

Tubas

Alfei Menashe

Qalqilya

Nablus

Ariel

Salfit

Eastern Segregation Zone

Modi'in Illit

Giv'at Ze'ev

Ramallah

Ma'ale Adumim

Jericho

Jerusalem

Gush Etzion

Bethlehem

Dead Sea

Kiryat Arba

Hebron

0 5 10 20
Kilometers

Rings of Israeli settlements, for example, cut off Jerusalem from the rest of the West Bank. This makes it more difficult for Palestinians to one day achieve their goal of an independent state with a shared Jerusalem as its capital. In addition, Israeli settlements and military outposts dominate the Jordan Valley and prevent Palestinian development there. Another set of Israeli settlements separates Bethlehem from Hebron, while still other settlements cut off Ramallah from Nablus.

Palestinians and Israelis committed to peace and reconciliation fear that the proliferation of settlements has already eliminated the possibility of establishing a viable, independent Palestinian state in the West Bank and Gaza Strip. Instead, settlement expansion is confining Palestinians to ever smaller parcels of land. This process, known by Palestinians as the cantonization or bantustanization of Palestine, is often compared to the establishment of Black homelands in South Africa under apartheid or the creation of Indian reservations for Native North Americans.

Since Israel has begun construction of a "separation barrier," the process of land confiscation is occurring faster than ever. The walls and fences of the separation barrier not only separate Israelis and Palestinians from each other, but also divide Palestinians from Palestinians and Palestinians from land, water, and other resources. The map on this page illustrates the route of the fences and walls that make it difficult at best for Palestinians to go from one part of Palestinian territory to another without hard-to-obtain Israeli permission. Meanwhile, Israel gains control of more and more of the West Bank and its natural resources such as water and land for agriculture and building.

An old man walks through Aida refugee camp in Bethlehem.

History

Im Munir and Abeer cook in the Odeh home in the Aida camp.

3. History

Who are the Palestinians?

Palestinians are Arabs who live in or come from the part of the Middle East today called Israel, the West Bank, and the Gaza Strip. Dispersal of Palestinians throughout the world makes an accurate count difficult, but researchers estimate that there are some 9.7 million Palestinians worldwide. Around 3.9 million Palestinians live in the West Bank and the Gaza Strip, with another 1.4 million living in Israel proper as citizens of the State of Israel. The rest live outside of Palestine-Israel in the diaspora.

At the beginning of the twentieth century, well over ninety percent of the people in Historical Palestine were Arabs. Historical Palestine was part of the Ottoman Empire, ruled from Istanbul in what is now Turkey. The Ottoman Empire extended from present-day Turkey down into what is now Saudi Arabia and over into Egypt in North Africa. During the late nineteenth and early twentieth centuries the peoples of the Middle East began to develop national identities. This process paralleled the development of European nationalities in the mid-eighteenth century. In practical terms, this meant that in the Middle East people began to think of themselves as Palestinians, Lebanese, Syrians, etc. There was as yet no State of Israel. The Jewish minority in the Middle East were also subjects of the Ottoman Empire.

After World War I, the lands of the defeated Ottoman Empire were divided up into different nations, kingdoms, and "mandate territories" by the League of Nations, the precursor of today's United Nations. The League of Nations gave Great Britain and France the mandate to administer various territories until they were deemed ready for democratic self-rule. France, for example, was given the mandate for

Lebanon and Syria, while Britain received the mandate for Palestine. This division of territory into various mandates accelerated the process of separate national identification. People in French-administered Syria, for example, began to view themselves as Syrians as well as Arabs, while those in British-administered Palestine viewed themselves more and more as Palestinians, in addition to being Arabs.

The process of Palestinian independence was complicated by the Balfour Declaration of 1917. This declaration committed Britain to working toward the creation of a Jewish homeland in Mandate Palestine. Palestinians interpreted the Balfour Declaration as evidence that the British authorities were not serious about moving Palestine along the path toward democracy and self-determination.

The Palestinian population at the turn of the twentieth century was 80 percent Muslim and 20 percent Christian. There were also Jewish communities in Palestine in Jerusalem, Hebron, Safed, and Tiberias which had been present for hundreds of years. These Jewish communities constituted about six percent of the total population of Historical Palestine and had made up about this percentage of the population for more than one thousand years. In the 1930s and 1940s Jewish communities in Mandate Palestine were joined by large numbers of immigrants from Europe.

By 1946 the Jewish population of Mandate Palestine had risen to 600,000, or about 33 percent of the total population. Also by this time some six percent of the land in Mandate Palestine was owned by Jews.

Today, Christians make up no more than two percent of the Palestinian population in the West Bank and Gaza Strip, and around eight percent of the Palestinians in Israel. The rest of the Palestinian population is Sunni Muslim. Many Palestinian Christians, along with upwardly mobile Palestinian Muslims, have emigrated to the North America and Europe in search of a life free of political oppression and economic uncertainty.

What is Zionism?

Zionism is the belief that Jews should have a state of their own. In late nineteenth century Europe a form of Zionism emerged which held that, just as the French people had France, or the Italians had Italy, the Jewish people should have a Jewish state. These early Zionists were almost all secular Jews. They viewed their Judaism as an ethnic and cultural characteristic rather than as a personal religious faith.

The father of this form of Zionism was the Austrian journalist Theodore Herzl, who wrote the landmark book *Der Judenstaat* (The Jewish State) outlining his vision of a new Jewish state of Israel. Herzl and his fellow Zionists dreamed of

establishing the Jewish state of Israel as a secular, socialist utopia. In the early days of Zionism, European Zionist leaders considered several locations for the new Jewish state, including parts of Uganda and Argentina. Palestine, however, quickly became the focus of Zionist aspirations, and groups of Zionist settlers began arriving in Palestine in the late nineteenth century. In contrast to these secular Jewish Zionists, most religious Jews opposed Zionism prior to the Holocaust on the grounds that only the Messiah could inaugurate a revived Jewish state.

Zionists argued that Jewish attempts to assimilate into the Christian West were doomed to failure. Jewish life would only be secure, Zionists believed, in a Jewish state. While many religious Jews initially opposed Zionism, the horrors of the Holocaust convinced many Jews that only a Jewish state would provide a safe haven for Jewish existence.

How was the State of Israel established? What was the Partition Plan?

In 1947, the United Nations passed General Assembly Resolution 181, otherwise known as the Partition Plan. This resolution divided Mandate Palestine into two parts. One section, comprising 56 percent of Mandate Palestine, was to be a Jewish state. The remaining 44 percent was to be a homeland for the native Palestinian Arab population. At the time of the Partition Plan, Jews owned six percent of the land in Mandate Palestine and Palestinians Arabs owned the remaining 94 percent. The Palestinians rejected this division, which they interpreted as the loss of 56 percent of their homeland.

On May 15, 1948, the Zionist leadership in Palestine, led by David Ben-Gurion, declared the creation of the State of Israel. This declaration ignited the war Israelis call "The War of Independence" and Palestinians call "The Catastrophe" (the Nakba in Arabic). Throughout this booklet the relatively neutral term "the War of 1948" designates this event. The Haganah and the Palmach, Jewish military units formed before the declaration of the State of Israel, fought against the armies of Egypt, Iraq, Jordan, and Syria, as well as military units of irregular Palestinian fighters. The Zionist armies proved better equipped and motivated, while the Arab states entered the war with conflicting motives and goals. During the course of the fighting between 700,000 to 900,000 Palestinians became homeless refugees, either because they fled in fear of the violence or were forcibly expelled by Israeli military forces. The Israeli military also destroyed over 500 Palestinian towns and villages. At the end of the war, Israel controlled 22 percent more land than originally called for in the Partition Plan, covering 78 percent of Mandate Palestine. The line separating the parties to the conflict came to be known as the 1949 Armistice Line, or, more commonly, the "Green Line."

What is the relationship between the Holocaust and the State of Israel?

The Holocaust, also known as the Shoah (the Hebrew word for destruction), refers to the systematic slaughter of millions of Jews and others throughout Europe during the Second World War. The Nazi ideology of Adolph Hitler viewed Jews and other "non-Aryans" as less-than-human and a threat to racial purity. Jewish people were rounded up, enslaved in concentration camps, killed in gas chambers, and cremated in what Nazis chillingly called "the Final Solution." Millions of other "unde-sirables" were imprisoned and killed in the camps, including Roma and Sinti people (more commonly known as Gypsies), people with mental and physical disabilities, homosexuals, pacifists, Communists, Jehovah's witnesses, and many other Christians. European Jews suffered the heaviest losses, with an estimated six million killed in the concentration camps.

The Holocaust, for many Jews, was a horrible confirmation of the Zionist argument that Jews would never be truly at home in Europe and that their security could only be guaranteed in a state of their own. Many religious Jews, who had previously opposed Zionism, understandably became dedicated Zionists after the Holocaust.

After World War II, many Jewish survivors of the Holocaust immigrated to Israel in search of a safe haven. Even for Jews who did not immigrate to Israel, merely the idea of Israel was comforting to many, as it promised safety in the event that genocidal, anti-Jewish forces gained power once more. Zionism, which had begun as a European movement seeking to colonize Palestine by displacing and ignoring local Palestinian Arabs, changed significantly after World War II. Unlike their predecessors, the Jews arriving from Europe after the Holocaust were not so much concerned with nation-building or the realization of a utopian vision as with safety and security from the ravages of genocide.

Almost 60 years later, the Holocaust continues to play a major role in discussions of the Palestine-Israel conflict. Some people believe that, given Western Christianity's shameful history of anti-Jewish discrimination and complicity in the Holocaust, Christians have no moral right to criticize the state of Israel. Others, however, suggest that past silence in the face of genocide should push Christians and others concerned with justice and peace to raise their voices whenever any government pursues policies of discrimination, exclusion and dispossession.

Who are the Palestinian refugees? Why are they still refugees? What is the Right of Return?

Around 7.2 million Palestinian refugees live around the world, of whom six million are either refugees from 1948 or their descendants. The remainder are internally displaced Palestinians inside Israel, Palestinians displaced during the 1967 war, and Palestinians displaced after 1967. An approximate 4.3 million Palestinians are registered as refugees with the United Nations Relief and Works Agency (UNRWA), the organization responsible for providing relief and basic services to Palestinian refugees. Only Palestinian refugees from the 1948 war who ended up outside of the new State of Israel were registered with UNRWA: Palestinian refugees who remained inside Israel ("internally displaced persons") were not able to register with UNRWA. Neither could Palestinians who lost their homes in the 1967 war or during the subsequent and ongoing occupation of the West Bank and the Gaza Strip.

Many Palestinian refugees live in refugee camps operated by UNWRA in the West Bank and Gaza Strip, Lebanon, Jordan and Syria. Camp residents do not live in tents; instead they have built small concrete block houses with rudimentary plumbing and electricity. The camps are extremely crowded and offer a low standard of living. Over the years, some refugees have moved out of the camps into neighboring residential areas, or have gone to live in other parts of the world.

In 1949 the United Nations passed the General Assembly Resolution 194. This resolution called for the return of and compensation for those refugees from the 1948 war willing to live at peace with their neighbors, and stipulated that the refugees be allowed back to their homes and properties at the earliest practicable date. As a condition for joining the United Nations, Israel had to affirm this resolution. Israel has, however, adamantly refused to allow any Palestinian refugees to return to their homes, and the resolution has never been enforced.

Some people believe it is logistically impossible for most Palestinian refugees to return to their original homes. Actually, most of the land to which refugees have the right to return is currently not being used for residential purposes, making it feasible for the majority of refugees to return to what is now Israel, if they so choose. Broadly understood, Israeli opposition to this process stems more fundamentally from a desire to minimize the Palestinian population of Israel rather than from any existential threat that refugee return would pose.

In addition to the refugees from 1948 who ended up outside the borders of the new State of Israel, millions of other Palestinians are refugees in the sense of having been displaced from their homes. "Internally displaced" Palestinians provide one example. These Palestinians lost their homes and lands in what became Israel in 1948, but remained inside Israel's newly-created borders. Archbishop Elias Chacour, the well-known Greek Catholic (Melkite) priest in the Galilee, originally came from the village of Bir'im in northern Galilee. In 1949, the Israeli military ordered the residents of Bir'im and neighboring Ikrit to leave their villages, promising them they

would be allowed to return. The military, however, proceeded to demolish the towns and prevented villagers from returning. Chacour and his fellow villagers, who are Israeli citizens, may not be included on United Nations lists of refugees, but like "official" refugees they lost their homes and lands. Still another group of Palestinian refugees is comprised of those who became homeless as a result of the

war in 1967, also known as the Six Day War.

After the War of 1948, Israel invoked a law known as the Absentee Property Law to take over Palestinian-owned properties left vacant when their owners became refugees or were internally displaced. The Custodian of Absentee Property, an Israeli government institution, allowed the Jewish National Fund (JNF), an agency to promote Jewish settlement in the land, to use many of these properties. Because the JNF allows only Jews to use its properties, much of the Palestinian land became a resource for exclusively Jewish development.

Although most of the original refugees have not seen their homes and properties since 1948, they continue to identify with the land from which they were expelled during the war. Many refugees still treasure the deeds to their land and carefully store the large iron keys to their original homes. Women continue to decorate their clothes with the embroidery patterns of their home villages. When refugee children born in the camps are asked where they are from, they typically name the cities and villages from which their grandparents came, places they have never seen, instead of the refugee camps in which they have lived all their lives.

What is the Law of Return?

The Law of Return is an Israeli law guaranteeing that any Jew can automatically become a citizen of the State of Israel. Furthermore, persons from some countries-in which organized Jewish life had not been possible, such as the countries of the former Soviet Union—can immigrate to Israel as gentiles if they have a Jewish grandparent. As an incentive to make aliyah (the Hebrew word for immigration to Israel), Israel offers generous immigration benefits to those who enter under the Law of Return. New immigrants are eligible for free (one-way) plane tickets, free and subsidized housing, no-interest loans, reduced taxes and tax exemptions, free medical insurance, free language study, and other attractive benefits.

Given the generosity of the new immigrant benefits package, it is perhaps not surprising that many recent immigrants to Israel are not Jewish. This is particularly true of immigrants from the former Soviet Union, who make up the vast majority of Israel's new immigrants. In 2001, for example, only half of all new immigrants identified themselves as Jewish upon entering the country, and nine percent identified themselves as Christians. Many of these immigrants come to Israel not for religious reasons, but in search of economic opportunities and hopes for a better life.

Israeli soldiers detain Palestinian teenagers in the streets of Hebron, West Bank.

The Law of Return and relatively recent amendments to it are hotly contested within Israeli society. Some defend a policy, crafted to bring in new immigrants from the former Soviet Union, that allows anyone with a Jewish grandparent to claim Israeli citizenship, arguing that Israel should provide safe haven for those the Nazis would have killed (anyone with a Jewish grandparent in Nazi Germany was in danger of being sent to the concentration camps). Other Israelis worry that by admitting so many immigrants who are not Jewish, or who lack a significant connection to Jewish identity and heritage, Israel is allowing its identity as a Jewish state to weaken. Still other Israelis welcome all immigration under the Law of Return because it increases the number and proportion of non-Arabs in Israel. These Israelis fear the high birthrate of Israel's minority Palestinian population, and seek to absorb as many non-Arabs as possible regardless of their religion.

Palestinian refugees find fundamentally unjust the contrast between Israel's refusal to implement their UN-mandated right of return and Israel's embrace of the Law of Return. In practice this means that Palestinian refugees who had been born in

Israel proper and then became refugees cannot enter Israel, while anyone born anywhere in the world who is Jewish can automatically become an Israeli citizen.

What is the Palestine Liberation Organization?

The Palestine Liberation Organization, commonly known as the PLO, was established in the early 1960s as the official organization of the Palestinian national independence movement. The PLO has traditionally functioned as the Palestinian government in exile, claiming to represent all Palestinians living in Palestine and in the diaspora. Yassir Arafat, the well-known Palestinian national leader, became chairman of the PLO in the mid-1960s. In 1996 Arafat was also elected the first president of the Palestinian Authority (see next page), a

An empty belt of 7.62mm light machine gun ammunition found by the Thalgieh family near the Israeli emplacement from which came the bullet that killed their son.

position he held until his death in the fall of 2004. Mahmoud Abbas (also called Abu Mazen) succeeded Arafat as the leader of the PLO after Arafat's death and was elected President of the Palestinian Authority in January 2005.

Traditionally most Palestinians have considered the PLO to be the only legitimate representative of the Palestinian people. Many political parties make up the PLO, including Fatah, the largest party, founded by Arafat and currently led by Abbas, the Popular Front for the Liberation of Palestine, and the Democratic Front for the Liberation of Palestine. Not all Palestinian political organizations belong to the PLO, however; neither Hamas nor Islamic Jihad (both revolutionary Islamic movements) is a PLO member.

What is the Occupation?

By the end of the war in 1948, Israel had taken control of 78 percent of Mandate Palestine. The remaining 22 percent was divided into two parts: the West Bank and the Gaza Strip. The West Bank, which included East Jerusalem and its Old City, was claimed by the Hashemite Kingdom of Jordan, while the Gaza Strip was administered by Egypt.

Then, during the "Six Day War" of 1967, Israeli military forces drove the Jordanians out of the West Bank and East Jerusalem and the Egyptians out of the Gaza Strip and began to occupy those areas militarily. Israel also conquered the Sinai Peninsula, which belonged to Egypt, and the Golan Heights, belonging to Syria. The Sinai was eventually returned to Egypt as part of the Camp David Accords of 1978. Israel officially annexed the Golan Heights and East Jerusalem, claiming them as integral parts of the state of Israel. The international community has refused to recognize these annexations as legitimate, and considers East Jerusalem and the Golan Heights to be Occupied Territories. The West Bank and the Gaza Strip were not annexed but remained under Israeli military control, a situation which persists to this day and is usually referred to as "the Occupation." [Even after Israel's withdrawal from the heart of the Gaza Strip in summer 2004, it continued to hold full control over all of the Strip's borders with the outside world, thus maintaining the occupation.] By occupying instead of annexing these territories, Israel avoided extending citizenship to the Palestinians of the West Bank and Gaza Strip, a move Israel feared would undermine the Jewish majority in Israel.

Israel argues that it is not occupying the West Bank and the Gaza Strip but is simply "administering" disputed territories. However, the international community, including the United States, Canada, the United Nations, and Israeli human rights organizations, agrees that Israel is in fact an occupying power. As such, Israel has obligations under international law (specifically the Fourth Geneva Convention, which Israel has signed) to safeguard the well-being of the civilian population in the territories it occupies, to avoid confiscating natural resources such as water from those territories, and to refrain from moving its own civilian population into the Occupied Territories.

Israel routinely violates the provisions of the Fourth Geneva Convention. For example, Israel fails to safeguard the well-being of the occupied Palestinian population when it collectively punishes the Palestinians of the West Bank and Gaza Strip with curfews, house demolitions, and closures (sieges) of Palestinian towns and villages. In addition, Israel routinely denies due process to Palestinian prisoners and illegally confiscates natural resources from the Occupied Territories, such as water from West Bank aquifers.

One of the most sobering elements of Israel's occupation policy is its construction of illegal settlements, also known as colonies, for Israeli civilians on confiscated Palestinian land. The Geneva Convention expressly forbids occupying powers to move any of their civilian population into Occupied Territories. This provision is intended to protect civilian populations who may be the targets of the anger of an occupied people. Because of Israel's multiple violations of the Forth Geneva Convention, its occupation of the West Bank and Gaza Strip is illegal in practice. Many jurists also argue that Israel's policy of maintaining an indefinite occupation makes the occupation itself illegal.

On November 22, 1967, the United Nations passed Security Council

The Israeli settlement of Har Homa built on Jebel Abu Ghneim, a mountain south of Jerusalem.

What are settlements?

The term "settlements" refers to the Israeli colonies established in the Occupied Territories. Some Palestinians and their advocates prefer the term "colonies" to "settlements" because it highlights the role of the settlements in controlling the land and natural resources of the Occupied Territories. As noted above, international law prohibits an occupying power from moving its civilians into occupied territory. This prohibition, however, has not deterred a series of Israeli governments, including the left-leaning Labor party, the right-leaning Likud party, and the centrist Kadima party, established by the former Israeli Prime Minister Ariel Sharon and currently led by the current Israeli Prime Minister Ehud Olmert. Israel began establishing settlements in the early 1970s and the number of settlers and settlements has steadily proliferated. Today there are nearly 200 settlements in the West Bank and East Jerusalem (not including 100 outposts deemed illegal even by the Israeli government) housing approximately 430,000 settlers.

Resolution (UNSCR) 242 calling on Israel to withdraw from territories occupied during the 1967 war in exchange for peace. This "land-for-peace" formula was the basis of the Egyptian-Israeli peace agreement brokered by Jimmy Carter and outlined in the Camp David Accords of 1978. (The Israel-Egypt Peace Treaty itself was signed in 1979). Exploiting an ambiguity in the resolution, Israel has argued that UNSCR 242 does not call on it to withdraw from all Occupied Territories, and so insists that its continued occupation of the West Bank and Gaza Strip does not constitute a violation of the resolution. Palestinians and Arab countries disagree, arguing that a just and lasting peace can only be achieved with a full Israeli withdrawal from all the territories occupied in 1967.

Settlements are typically built on land confiscated from Palestinians. Sometimes the Israeli government uses Ottoman-era land laws as a pretext for expropriating land from Palestinian landowners. Other times the land is simply taken. Sometimes Palestinians are coerced into selling, or sell fearing that the land will end up being confiscated while they are left with nothing. The subsequent building of settlements results in more than a loss of land. Israel strategically positions settlements in order to secure control over water from West Bank and Gaza Strip aquifers.

Another function of Israeli settlement policy is to gain control over Palestinian population centers by establishing geographical control. Palestinians, for example, have always considered Jerusalem to be their capital. They envision Jerusalem as an international city that can be the shared capital of two states and two peoples. In contrast, Israeli governments have opposed the idea of sharing Jerusalem, insisting that the city be entirely for Israel. In order to make this desire a practical reality, Israel has created "facts on the ground" by establishing settlements in a pattern that encircles Palestinian neighborhoods in East Jerusalem. These settlements effectively isolate Palestinian neighborhoods from each other, and cut off East Jerusalem from the West Bank. This settlement policy undermines the possibility of any political settlement that includes a real

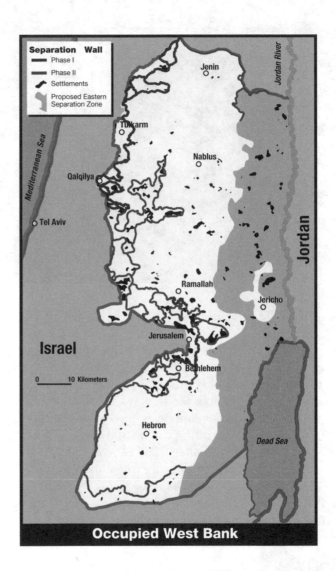

Separation Wall
— Phase I
— Phase II
➤ Settlements
▨ Proposed Eastern Separation Zone

Mediterranean Sea

Jordan River

Jenin

Tulkarm

Nablus

Qalqilya

Tel Aviv

Jordan

Ramallah

Jericho

Jerusalem

Israel

Bethlehem

0   10 Kilometers

Hebron

Dead Sea

Occupied West Bank

A candle sits next to a photo of the mother of Joseph Thalgieh. She died after inhaling tear gas during the first intifada of the 1980s.

sharing of Jerusalem as one city, two capitals.

Israel employs a similar settlement strategy throughout the West Bank. Settlements in these territories are established in ways that eliminate territorial contiguity for Palestinians, separating town from town and village from village. This leaves Palestinians unable to move from one Palestinian town to the next without passing through Israeli-controlled territory. In addition, over the past decade Israel has built a network of special roads connecting the settlements to each other. Land for the roads has been appropriated from Palestinian territory, and the right of Palestinians to use these roads is tightly restricted. Once again, the practical implication of this policy is to undermine any political settlement that involves the creation of a viable Palestinian state, as Palestinian towns and cities have been separated by a sprawling network of settlements and settlement roads.

Some Israeli settlers are motivated by political and religious beliefs, convinced, for example, that settling the whole of Eretz Yisrael (Hebrew phrase for the Land of Israel) is a sacred obligation. They believe that Jews are destined to subjugate, if not displace entirely, native Palestinian inhabitants. The majority of settlers, however, choose life in the settlements for economic reasons: the Israeli government offers a variety of incentives for Israelis to live in settlements, including tax breaks and low- to no-interest mortgages.

What is the separation barrier?

For Palestinians and their international advocates one of the most alarming developments in Israel's West Bank construction activities is the building of the separation barrier. Some Israelis believe that this barrier will bring freedom from suicide bombings and other violent acts. As is usual in Palestine-Israel the different names used to refer to the same entity reveal the tremendous difference in perspectives found in this conflict. The barrier, called a "security fence" by Israel, but known by Palestinians as the "apartheid wall" or the "segregation wall" is designed to enable Israel to solidify control over a maximum amount of West Bank territory while absorbing a minimal number of Palestinians. The walls and fences of the separation barrier are means of enforcing separation through force. At points, the barrier is a concrete wall that reaches nearly thirty feet in height and features a series of guard towers. In other areas, the barrier is an elaborate series of fences, barbed wire, roads and electronic sensors.

Whether an electronic fence or a concrete wall, the barrier is walling off Palestinians from Israelis, walling off Palestinians from Palestinians, and walling off Palestinians from agricultural land, water, education, religious sites, and social services. The wall is not in fact being built on Israel's Green Line border with the West Bank. Instead, land for the wall is being confiscated from the West Bank communities it is designed to isolate, and may eventually result in the annexation of at least ten percent of the West Bank to Israel. Some Palestinian population centers, such as Qalqilya in the north, are almost entirely encircled by the wall. The walls and fences in effect annex land and water resources (along with many settlements) to Israel, while leaving Palestinians encircled in reservations that many observers liken to the Bantustans of apartheid-era South Africa.

When completed, the separation barrier will reach nearly 700 km in length. Up to 80 percent of the barrier is being built inside the occupied West Bank, with only 20 percent built on or near the Green Line. The separation barrier, together with Israeli settlements and the network of roads linking settlements with each other and with Israel, is an integral part of Israel's "convergence" or "unilateral separation" plan. In this plan, Israel seeks to deepen its control over a maximum amount of West Bank territory while "disengaging" itself from a maximum number of Palestinians, leaving them trapped behind the walls and fences of the separation barrier.

In July 2004 the International Court of Justice (the ICJ) ruled that the separation barrier violated international law. The ICJ ruling called for the dismantling of the walls and fences already constructed and the compensation of Palestinians whose lands and properties had been damaged during its construction. Israel has ignored the ICJ ruling, and the international community has not exerted any pressure on Israel to adhere to it.

What was the first intifada?

Throughout the 1970s and the early part of the 1980s, foreign reporters visiting the West Bank and the Gaza Strip routinely commented on how quiet the Palestinian population was, given their suffering at the hands of Israeli policy. This apparent quiet masked deep-seated frustration and anger at life under military occupation and at the expanding Israeli settlement enterprise. On December 9, 1987, the quiet gave way to protest as Palestinians in the Gaza Strip launched the intifada, the resistance movement that quickly spread to the West Bank and East Jerusalem. Intifada is an Arabic word that literally means "shaking off," but is commonly translated as "uprising." The first intifada, which lasted until 1993, inspired ordinary Palestinians to engage in nonviolent resistance to the Israeli military authorities, particularly during the uprising's first years. Palestinians used nonviolent tactics such as strikes, tax resistance and unarmed demonstrations designed to "shake off" the Israeli occupation and express their desire to live in freedom. The movement was not entirely nonviolent, however: stone-throwing

Palestinian youth and, especially later in the intifada, groups of armed fighters also participated in the uprising.

The Israeli military responded harshly to the intifada. Yitzhak Rabin, then Israeli Defense Minister and later Prime Minister and Nobel Laureate, famously promised to "crush the bones" of those taking part in the uprising. The first intifada drew to a close with the announcement of the Declaration of Principles and the signing of what came to be known as the Oslo Accords.

What were the Oslo Accords?

In September of 1993, the PLO and the State of Israel issued a Declaration of Principles (DOP), the product of secret negotiations conducted in the Norwegian capital of Oslo. The DOP set the general framework for the more detailed "Oslo Accords" that would follow. In the Oslo Accords, the PLO recognized the existence and legitimacy of the State of Israel. Israel, for its part, simply recognized the PLO as a representative of the Palestinian people, something they had denied until this time. The Gaza-Jericho First Agreement (also known as Oslo I) gave Palestinians "autonomy" over the West Bank town of Jericho and about 60% of the Gaza Strip. The Cairo Agreement (or Oslo II) extended Palestinian autonomy into additional parts of the West Bank. Oslo II divided the West

An Israeli soldier checks the documents of a Palestinian teenager.

Bank into a geographical alphabet soup. In Area A, comprising the main cities of the West Bank, Palestinians had control over civilian and security affairs. In Area B, which included villages near Palestinian cities, Palestinians had responsibility for civil services such as schools and hospitals while Israel remained in control of security. In Area C, meanwhile, Israel retained full control.

In order to fulfill the requirements of the Area A, B, and C system, the Oslo Accords established joint Palestinian-Israeli coordination mechanisms for security and stipulated a series of three Israeli withdrawals. At the end of these withdrawals Israel was to have pulled back from all of the Occupied Territories except for settlements and designated military areas. Palestinians understood this provision to mean that, after the three Israeli withdrawals, the Palestinian Authority would be in control of 95 percent of the West Bank. Only two withdrawals were carried out, however, and these withdrawals occurred only after delays and prolonged negotiations. After the second withdrawal was carried out in 1999, still only 18 percent of the West Bank fell under full Palestinian control (Area A); in another 22 percent Palestinians had responsibility for civilian affairs while Israel maintained responsibility for security (Area B); in the remaining 60 percent of the West Bank Israel kept full control (Area C). Palestinian-controlled territories (be it Areas A or B) lacked territorial contiguity, broken up by Israeli-controlled land (Area C).

The Oslo Accords were based on the principle that the most contentious issues of the Palestine-Israel conflict, referred to as the "final status" issues, would be deferred to a second phase of negotiations which would take place five years later. These final status issues included: the future of Israeli settlements in the Occupied Territories; the use of water resources in the Occupied Territories; the fate of Palestinian refugees; the final status of Jerusalem; and the final borders of a

MCC peace development worker Ed Nyce and Ruti al-Raz, International Coordinator for the Israeli Committee Against House Demolitions (ICAHD), tour and discuss the separation wall in the Abu Dis neighborhood of East Jerusalem.

Palestinian state. In the meantime, the three Israeli withdrawals and the negotiations on the final status issues were to be completed during the course of a five year "interim phase." This interim phase expired on May 31, 1999, with most of these goals unmet.

Supporters of the Oslo process argued that it was impossible to reach agreement on all of the difficult issues affecting Palestinians and Israelis. They maintained that the only way forward was to postpone those issues and hope that a series of incremental measures would foster a spirit of trust and mutuality that would allow for the resolution of those issues at a future date. Critics of the Oslo Accords, in contrast, claimed that an incremental process served the interests of the stronger party to the negotiations, namely Israel. They pointed out that the Oslo Accords

were vague about the timing and extent of the stipulated Israeli withdrawals and that they lacked any enforcement mechanism. These critics also noted that this ambiguity, combined with the postponement of the most difficult negotiations, would allow Israel, as the stronger party, to consolidate its grip on the Occupied Territories rather than take steps to withdraw from them. Unfortunately, it appears that criticisms of Oslo were justified. The Israeli authorities not only repeatedly delayed withdrawals from parts of the West Bank, they also accelerated settlement building in the Occupied Territories, established new settlements, expanded existing ones, and constructed a network of "bypass roads" to connect settlements with one another. The number of Israeli settlers in the Occupied Territories nearly doubled during the Oslo years.

By the time Oslo's "interim phase" expired at the end of May 1999, Palestinians had gone from an enthusiastic embrace of the Oslo Accords to a mood of pessimism and despair. It had become apparent to the Palestinians and their supporters that the Oslo Accords had not been about ending the occupation, but about solidifying Israel's control over the Occupied Territories. The accords allowed Israel to free itself of the mundane obligations of an occupying power, such as operating schools and hospitals and safeguarding the wellbeing of civilians, while retaining control over the majority of the Occupied Territories.

Critics of the Oslo Accords also noted that the incremental nature of the accords allowed the process to be held hostage by extremist organizations. A minority of Palestinians, mainly supporters of groups such as Hamas, Islamic Jihad and the Popular Front for the Liberation of Palestine, favored continued armed struggle over the Oslo Accords. When members of these groups carried out a suicide bombing or other violent attack, Israel typically cited the violence as a reason to discontinue the withdrawals mandated by Oslo. Palestinians opposed to Oslo recognized this dynamic and used it to further their own interests, much to the chagrin of the majority of Palestinians who were at least initially Oslo supporters.

What is the Palestinian Authority?

The Palestinian Authority (PA) was set up as part of the Oslo agreements. While not a sovereign government, the Palestinian Authority is, according to the Oslo Accords, responsible for civilian and security affairs in parts of the West Bank and the Gaza Strip. The PA has disappointed the many Palestinians who rejoiced in its creation as the first step toward the establishment of the long-awaited independent Palestinian state. Instead of ushering in a new era of Palestinian self-determination, the PA has become barely functional. Israeli-imposed closures of the West Bank and Gaza Strip have severely restricted Palestinian movement between population centers by means of roadblocks and checkpoints. Israel's reinvasions of Palestinian cities have further weakened the PA. Because of the geographical fragmentation created by Israeli military measures, the PA is unable to operate as an effective national body—the various PA ministries are basically extensions of municipalities and village councils. Corruption within the PA has also weakened its status in the eyes of average Palestinians.

Some Palestinians and Israelis have observed that the existence of the Palestinian Authority allows Israel to maintain its occupation of the West Bank and the Gaza Strip, without taking responsibility for the welfare of the civilian population, as required under international law. Instead, the international community, through its support of the Palestinian Authority and through emergency relief to the Occupied Territories, ends up funding the occupation.

In January 2006, Hamas, the main Islamist party in the Occupied Territories, won a majority of seats in the Palestinian Legislative Council. In response, most of the international donor governments suspended assistance to the PA. Most observers credited Hamas' victory to the failure of the PA to achieve tangible political gains in negotiations with Israel and to the Palestinian public's frustration with corruption within the PA. Political analysts observed that Hamas' victory was more a protest vote against Fatah's corruption and incompetence than a widespread endorsement of Islamist politics.

While the international donor community suspended direct aid to the PA, it continued to provide indirect support to Palestinian institutions through the United Nations and other mechanisms. Neither the international community nor Israel wished for the PA to collapse, as the PA's continued existence relieved Israel of its responsibility under international law for the welfare of the civilian population in the Occupied Territories.

What is the Al-Aqsa Intifada?

On September 30, 2000, a second uprising against Israeli occupation began, this time known as the Al-Aqsa Intifada. This new intifada received its name from the Al-Aqsa Mosque, part of the Noble Sanctuary in Jerusalem's Old City.

On September 28, 2000, Ariel Sharon, who was then leader of Israel's opposition Likud party, visited this Muslim holy site in the company of hundreds of armed Israeli soldiers and police. This provocative move asserted Israeli control over the Muslim holy site. The following day Israeli military units opened fire on Palestinians around the Al-Aqsa mosque who were protesting Sharon's visit of the day before. Five Palestinians were killed and more than 200 were injured. These killings inspired waves of protest by Palestinians, both within Israel and in the Occupied Territories. During the month of October 2000, 13 Palestinian citizens of Israel were killed by Israeli police during demonstrations in Palestinian towns in Israel. Scores of Palestinians in the Occupied Territories were also killed, and thousands more injured. By the end of July 2006, more than 4,100 Palestinians had been killed by Israeli soldiers and settlers. More than 30,500 Palestinians, meanwhile, had been injured. Israelis have also been the targets of Palestinian violence in the Al-Aqsa Intifada. More than 1,000 Israelis have

Itay Nachliel and Ruti al-Raz discuss the wall. Nachliel is an engineer living in Tel Aviv who believes the wall is necessary for Israeli security and to prevent terrorism, but is troubled by the way in which it has been implemented.

been killed and around 7,600 more have been injured. Sadly, the killing and violence continue.

Why was there a second Intifada? Didn't the Palestinians turn down a generous offer at Camp David in July 2000?

The five-year interim period established by the Oslo Accords expired in May 1999 without a completion of Israeli withdrawals from the Occupied Territories and without the start of negotiations on final status issues. Meanwhile, peace negotiations continued to limp along, hindered by Israeli settlement expansion and Palestinian suicide bombings. Eventually, in July of 2000, then President of the United States, Bill Clinton, called together Yassir Arafat, then chairman of the PLO and president of the Palestinian Authority, and Ehud Barak, then Israeli Prime Minister, for a summit at Camp David.

Clinton hoped the summit would produce a dramatic breakthrough in the stalemated negotiations, a breakthrough that would address outstanding final status issues. The outcome of the summit is not in question: the United States was unable to generate a Palestinian-Israeli agreement. The substance of the summit, however, remains hotly debated. The various parties do not agree on what proposals were or weren't made, and who should take the blame for the summit's failure. Israeli officials accused the Palestinians of having rejected the most generous Israeli offer ever, claiming that Israel offered the Palestinians 90 percent of the West Bank. Some reports from the summit indicate that Israel did discuss withdrawing from between 80 to 90 percent of West Bank territory, albeit territory that would have been broken up by Israeli settlement blocs that Israel would have annexed. In contrast, Palestinian sources at the summit

Palestinians who believed that they had already made the far larger concession when they relinquished 78 percent of Mandate Palestine to the State of Israel and accepted establishing a Palestinian state in the remaining 22 percent.

Some Israeli officials and their international supporters claimed that the Palestinian leadership, having failed to obtain what it wanted through negotiations, turned to violence and launched the second intifada, the Al-Aqsa Intifada. Other analysts, including Palestinians and their Israeli and international supporters, paint a different picture. They locate the outbreak of the Al-Aqsa Intifada against the backdrop of years of popular frustration with a peace process that was neither ending the occupation nor improving the economic situation for the average Palestinian. In this view the visit by Ariel Sharon to the Haram al-Sharif (the Noble Sanctuary) was simply a spark that ignited an already volatile situation. Immediately after the Sharon visit the Palestinian Authority might have been able to calm the Palestinian population. But the heavy-handed Israeli response to the initial demonstrations, a response that left scores dead, further inflamed Palestinian public sentiment. The Palestinian leadership, rather than instigating the second intifada, played the role of follower.

have questioned the extent of the alleged Israeli compromises.

What is clear is that Palestinian and Israeli negotiators approached discussions about the borders of a future Palestinian state from very different angles. Palestinians believed they had already made their major concession when they signed the Oslo Accords and agreed to give up the 78 percent of Mandate Palestine which is today the State of Israel. From the Palestinian perspective, the point of the Camp David negotiations was to discuss how to end Israel's occupation of the remaining 22 percent of Mandate Palestine. Israel, on the other hand, viewed the negotiations as centering on what portion of that remaining 22 percent would be retained by the state of Israel, and how much of it would be relinquished to the Palestinians. What Israel portrayed as a generous offer did not feel generous to

What is the Road Map?

The Road Map refers to the path to peace in Palestine-Israel as envisioned by the George W. Bush administration. The second Gulf War of 2003 confirmed the suspicions of many in the Middle East that the United States favored Israel and discriminated against Arab countries. In an effort to allay these suspicions and promote the idea that the United States could play the role of Middle Eastern peacemaker as well as warrior, the Bush administration laid out the plan known as the Road Map.

The Road Map, like the Oslo Accords, involves incremental stages. Unlike the Oslo Accords, however, it insists that the two parties, Israeli and Palestinian, must move together simultaneously, not conditioning their actions on the actions of the other party. In the first phase of the Road Map, Palestinians are to reactivate security services (which had been decimated by the Israeli military, a fact not mentioned in the Road Map) and to act against Palestinian militant networks. Israel, meanwhile, is to freeze settlement construction and to dismantle settlement outposts that even Israel acknowledges to be illegal. By the end of the first phase, a provisional Palestinian state is to be established in parts of the Occupied Territories—most likely no more than 40 percent of the West Bank and 60

percent of the Gaza Strip. Like in the Oslo Accords, the core issues of the Palestinian-Israeli conflict (refugees, Jerusalem, settlements, etc.) are postponed to the final stages of negotiations.

While the Road Map is an improvement on the Oslo Accords in that it calls for an end to the occupation and envisions a viable Palestinian state next to Israel, most observers, be they peacebuilders, diplomats, aid workers, or others, view the Road Map as a dead letter. As Israel continues building its separation barrier throughout the West Bank, any Palestinian state that would emerge would not be viable, but would instead consist of disconnected cantons. When Palestinians and their advocates speak about ending the occupation, they mean a full withdrawal from the West Bank, East Jerusalem, and the Gaza Strip. When Israeli Prime Minister Ariel Sharon spoke of "ending the occupation" in a much-publicized speech in May 2003, he meant withdrawing from Palestinian population centers. The Road Map has not led to a real end of the occupation but rather to its solidification.

What is the unilateral separation (convergence) plan?

The former Israeli Prime Minister Ariel Sharon began the process of "unilateral separation" with the construction of the separation barrier and the withdrawal of

Abed Jabber stands in front of his bullet-riddled home in Azza refugee camp in Bethlehem.

Israeli troops and settlers from the heart of the Gaza Strip. Sharon's successor as Prime Minister, Ehud Olmert, has pledged to continue this process of separation, which he calls "convergence," with promises of unspecified withdrawals from parts of the West Bank in the future.

While some commentators initially hoped that unilateral Israeli withdrawals from parts of the Occupied Territories would be the first step toward a durable two-state solution to the Palestinian-Israeli conflict, as the plan has progressed such hopes have faded. An advisor to former

Israeli Primer Minister Sharon famously declared that the unilateral separation plan was designed to put the peace process "in formaldehyde." Before he became Prime Minister, Ehud Olmert described the process of unilateral separation as one of creating a reality with "Maximum land, minimum Palestinians." Palestinian and Israeli peacebuilders fear that rather than setting the stage for a future reconciliation between Palestinians and Israelis, the unilateral separation plan is in fact a way for Israel to solidify and deepen its control over the Occupied Territories.

Samir Odeh shows where in the Qur'an it describes Ramadan and breaking the daily fast.

Religion

4. Religion

What religious beliefs are shared by Christians, Jews and Muslims? Do members of these three faiths all believe in the same God?

Christians, Jews and Muslims all believe in the same God. Jews encounter God in the Torah (the first five books of the Christian Bible), the Tanakh (the Torah, the prophetic books of the Bible, and wisdom writings such as Proverbs), and the Talmud (rabbinic commentary on the Torah). Christians encounter God in the Old Testament, the New Testament, and above all in the life, death, and resurrection of Jesus Christ. Muslims encounter God through the Qur'an.

These three faiths are often referred to as the three monotheistic faiths, or the three Abrahamic faiths. The latter expression refers to the patriarch Abraham who is a key figure in the traditions of all three religions. Jews and Christians trace the Abrahamic tradition through Abraham's wife Sarah and their son Isaac. Muslims also claim the tradition of Abraham, whom they call "the friend of God." Muslims trace the Abrahamic tradition through Abraham's concubine Hagar and their son Ishmael.

Christians, Muslims, and Jews call God by different names depending on their native languages, but all of these terms refer to the same God. In Arabic, the word for God is "Allah." Arabic speaking Christians and Muslims both refer to God by this name. Because the Qur'an was revealed in Arabic, some Muslims refer to God by using the Arabic name "Allah" when they are speaking English or other non-Arabic languages. Other Muslims use the name "God" in English contexts. Both of these options refer to the one God worshipped by members of all three Abrahamic faiths. This is similar to the way Spanish-speakers call God "Dios" or French speakers call God "Dieu," without referring to different deities.

Jewish God-talk is sometimes more complicated than that of Christians and Muslims, but it still designates the same Supreme Being. Jews refer to God in different ways depending on their religious orientation. Some Jews believe that the name God is so holy it cannot be spoken. To avoid pronouncing the Hebrew word for God, which is "Yahweh," they call God "HaShem," meaning "the Name." When writing in English, these Jews sometimes spell God without the "o," as in "G-d," in order to avoid direct reference to the sacred name. In general conversation, some Jews also use terms like "Adonai," meaning "the Lord," or "Elohim," meaning "the highest" when they refer to God. Many other Jews simply use the name "God" when speaking of God in English. Once again, all of these terms are ways of referring to the one God worshipped by Christians, Muslims and Jews.

One of the most important principles to remember in discussing different religions is that theory should be compared with theory and practice should be compared with practice. Christianity, Judaism and Islam all share an ethic of treating others fairly, yet all of these religions have adherents who fail to follow this general principle. In this sense, it is unfair to make comments like: "Christians believe in loving their enemies, but Muslims carry out acts of terrorism." In reality, both Christians and Muslims are enjoined to avoid violence, and both Christians and Muslims sometimes commit violence. It is also unfair to make comments like: "Islam is a religion of justice, but Jews and Christians are always violating the rights of Muslims." In truth, Judaism, Christianity and Islam all have strong traditions of justice, and Jews, Christians, and Muslims all sometimes violate human rights.

What beliefs and practices are unique to Christianity?

The foundation of Christianity is the belief that God, the creator of heaven and earth, was incarnated, took flesh in the person of Jesus Christ, who was born, conducted his ministry, then was crucified and resurrected. Christians believe that through Christ's atoning work humanity's reconciliation with God is made possible and real. Through God's Holy Spirit, creation is sustained and the church is empowered to live out its witness to God's love. Christians learn about the life of Jesus by reading the Bible. Both the Old Testament and the New Testament are sacred Christian scriptures. Christians worship God in churches through the reading of scripture, music, teaching, and prayer. Mennonites believe that a core element of Christianity is the rejection of violence. Along with other Christians, Mennonites believe in witnessing to the good news of the Gospel through love of God, neighbor and enemy.

What beliefs and practices are unique to Judaism?

Judaism, the oldest of the three monotheistic religions, is based on the Torah, the Jewish name for the Pentateuch, the first five books of the Hebrew Bible. (The Old Testament is often referred to as the Hebrew Bible in discussions of Judaism.) Jews also acknowledge the rest of the Old Testament as scripture. The Talmud, an extensive commentary on the Torah, is another important source of religious authority in Judaism.

Since Christians and Jews share the Old Testament, members of both faiths acknowledge the same Old Testament prophets. Jews are expected to follow the Ten Commandments as handed down by Moses. While Jews respect Jesus as a teacher, they reject his divinity. A small portion of persons of Jewish heritage do acknowledge the divinity of Jesus. Some of these call themselves "Christians of Jewish origin." Others prefer to be referred to as "Messianic Jews," and see Judaism as being completed by the divine Jesus. Observing Shabbat, the Hebrew term for the Sabbath, is an important practice for observant Jews. According to Jewish law, the Sabbath begins on Friday evening and continues until Saturday night. It is commonly believed that Jews are forbidden to work on Shabbat. A more complete understanding of the prohibition is that Jews are to refrain from creating or destroying anything on Shabbat in honor of the Creator God. This refers to everything from burning trash to activating an electrical current. In practice this means that observant Jews will not turn lights, TV, or radio on or off, use electrical appliances, write, drive a car, take a bus, or tie or untie a permanent knot on Shabbat. Shabbat time is often spent on religious activities such as attending services at a synagogue, or visiting friends and relatives.

In addition to "keeping Shabbat," observant Jews also "keep kosher," the phrase used to designate eating only foods permissible under Jewish law. Pork products and shellfish are forbidden. Fish, some birds, and land mammals with cloven hooves that chew their cuds are permitted. Keeping kosher also means keeping meat (flesh

Praying at the Wailing Wall in the Old City of Jerusalem.

from birds and mammals) and dairy foods separate. This means not eating such foods together at the same meal and keeping two sets of dishes, one for meat and one for dairy. Utensils that have come into contact with dairy cannot be used with meat and vice versa. Prohibiting meat and dairy combinations means, among other things, that observant Jews will never eat cheeseburgers or have meat on a pizza. Not all Jews are equally observant. According to Jewish law a Jew is anyone born to a Jewish mother or anyone who converts to Judaism. This means that Judaism has a quasi-ethnic quality. The majority of Jews in Israel, about 60 percent, are secular Jews. These are Jews who do not have a religious faith but who consider themselves Jewish for reasons of ethnic heritage and culture.

What beliefs and practices are unique to Islam?

Islam, the youngest of the three monotheistic faiths, is founded on the belief that God revealed the Holy Qur'an to the prophet Muhammad in Saudi Arabia in the seventh century CE. Many people erroneously assume that the Qur'an plays a role equivalent to the Bible in Christianity, and that Muhammad plays a role similar to Jesus. A better understanding of Islam acknowledges the Muslim belief that Muhammad was a human being but the Qur'an, containing the words of God, is a book of divine origin. Muslims do not worship the prophet Muhammad the way that Christians worship Jesus Christ. Muslims believe in the Old Testament prophets, they believe that Jesus was a prophet, and they believe that Muhammad is God's final prophet. They do not, however, worship any prophet, all of whom they consider fully and only human. In Islam, the concept of divinity is

Samir Odeh prays before breaking the Ramadan fast.

reserved for God alone. Devout Muslims pray in mosques on Fridays, the Islamic holy day. They also follow Islamic dietary restrictions, including abstaining from all alcohol and pork products.

Muslims are enjoined to follow the "Five Pillars" of Islam. These include:

- **Salah** *(Arabic word for prayer)*: Muslims are required to pray five times a day. During prayer they recite an Arabic text and perform a series of prostrations. They also engage in personal prayers and devotions at other times.

- **Zakat** *(Arabic word for alms)*: Muslims are required to give annually to the poor 2.5 percent of all they own. (Note that this is not 2.5 percent of their earnings, but rather 2.5 percent of all their possessions.)

- **Shehadah** *(Arabic word for witness)*: In this context, the Shehadah refers to the statement: "I will be a witness that there is no god but God and Muhammad is the prophet of God." A person becomes Muslim by speaking this phrase.

- **The Hajj** *(Arabic word for pilgrimage)*: All Muslims with the means to do so are required to make a pilgrimage once in their lifetime to the holy cities of Makkah and Medina in Saudi Arabia.

- **Ramadan** *(The name of the ninth month in the Islamic calendar)*: During the month of Ramadan Muslims fast during all daylight hours. This fast includes abstaining from food, drink, smoking, and sexual relations. In the evening Muslims break the fast as they gather to eat with family and friends. Ramadan is a time when Muslims are particularly conscious of their faith and put extra effort in strengthening family and community relationships.

What is the religious significance of Palestine-Israel? What special associations does this land hold for Jews, Christians, and Muslims?

Palestine-Israel is drenched in religious associations. Christians, Muslims and Jews all consider Palestine-Israel a holy land. Often the same religious site resonates deeply with more than one faith.

Judaism: For religious Jews, Palestine-Israel is Eretz Yisrael, a holy land promised by God to the Jewish people. The land is connected to Jewish history: Abraham and Sarah, Isaac and Rebecca, and Jacob and Leah are believed to be buried in the West Bank town of Hebron. Their graves are located in the Ibrahimi Mosque (al-Haram al-Ibrahimi in Arabic), known to Jews as the Cave of Machpelah. The matriarch Rachel is buried near Bethlehem where she died in childbirth. The kingdoms of David and Solomon flourished in what is now Palestine-Israel, and the temples of Solomon and Herod were built in Jerusalem.

The most sacred place in Judaism, the Western Wall, is found in the Old City of Jerusalem. Jews have gathered at the Western Wall, the only remaining support wall of the Second Temple, since the destruction of the Temple in 70 CE. There they lament the destruction of the temple, giving rise to the alternate name "the Wailing Wall."

Although religious Jews believe that Eretz Yisrael has been promised to them by God, the consensus among Jews until the mid-twentieth century was that the Jewish people would only be returned to the land at the coming of the Messiah. As a result, contemporary attempts to establish a Jewish state in historical Palestine were viewed as blasphemous, a belief still held by many ultra-Orthodox Jews. Other religious Jews, however, believe they are divinely mandated to settle all of Eretz Yisrael. These Jews argue that settling the land will help bring about the coming of the Messiah. Some Jews who hold this view are already at work preparing the implements to be used in the Third Temple, such as the type of priestly garments prescribed in Exodus 28 in the Old Testament. The most extreme proponents of this view believe that the Islamic holy site the Noble Sanctuary which houses the Dome of the Rock and the Al-Aqsa Mosque must be destroyed so the temple can be rebuilt in its place. Most religious Jews, however, refuse to enter the Temple Mount/Haram al-Sharif, fearful that they would inadvertently tread on the Holy of Holies, the section of the temple reserved for the High Priest.

Christianity: Palestine-Israel holds deep associations for Christians, not only from the stories of the Old Testament but especially from Jesus' birth, ministry, death and resurrection. The Church of the Nativity is found in Bethlehem, built over caves where Jesus was born. The Shepherds' Fields in Beit Sahour next to Bethlehem mark where angels appeared to announce Jesus' birth. In Galilee, in what is now northern Israel, churches have been built commemorating Jesus' teaching ministry around the Sea of Galilee. The Basilica of the Annunciation in Nazareth, a primarily Palestinian city in Israel proper, marks the proclamation of Jesus' conception to Mary by the angel Gabriel. Meanwhile, in Jerusalem's Old City, pilgrims retrace the steps of Jesus on the Via Dolorosa, the way of sorrows. This path leads to the Church of the Holy Sepulcher, a church that contains Gologtha, the site of Jesus' crucifixion, as well as the empty tomb in which Jesus' body was placed after his death and from which he arose on Easter morning. In addition to the dozens of churches and shrines commemorating biblical events, Palestine-Israel is also home to thousands of faithful Christians who have been living and worshipping in the land since the days of the early church.

Islam: For Muslims, Jerusalem is revered first and foremost as the site of the

Armenian Easter at the tomb of Jesus in Jerusalem at the Holy Sepulcher.

Prophet Muhammad's Night Journey. Pious Muslims have for centuries understood the Qur'an to describe a journey to "the farthest mosque" in which Muhammad rode from Saudi Arabia to Jerusalem on a winged horse named al-Buraq and from there ascended to heaven. Al-Aqsa, a name meaning "the farthest," is thus the name given to the mosque on the Haram al-Sharif (the Noble Sanctuary), the Muslim sanctuary built on the hilltop where the Jewish Temple once stood. Muslims consider the wall to which the steed was tied to be part of the sanctuary—and therefore as Islamic-endowed religious property, known as *waqf* in

Arabic. This wall also happens to be the Western Wall, the holiest site in Judaism where Jews gather to remember the Temple. Also in the Noble Sanctuary is the Qubbet al-Sakhrah, known in English as the Dome of the Rock. This stunning shrine was built in the eighth century over the rock that Islamic tradition associates with Abraham's near-sacrifice of his son, Ishmael. (The Qur'an teaches that God commanded Abraham to sacrifice his son Ishmael, not his son Isaac as recorded in the Old Testament.)

For centuries Muslims have referred to all of Jerusalem as Bayt al-Maqdas, or the House of the Holy. One mosque outside of Jerusalem with particular significance for Muslims is the Haram al-Ibrahimi, or Abraham's Sanctuary, in the West Bank city of Hebron. This resting place of the Old Testament matriarchs and patriarchs is important to Christians, Jews and Muslims. The site consists of a large building which contains a mosque and, more recently, a synagogue. (Jews refer to the site as the Cave of Machpelah.)

Are all Jews Zionists? Are all Zionists Jews?

Not all Jews are Zionists, and not all Zionists are Jews. Zionism began as a secular movement and was initially opposed by religious Jews. While the profound shock of the Holocaust caused many religious Jews to view the new State of Israel as a safe haven, many other religious Jews continued to find the Zionist project of establishing a Jewish state sacrilegious. Other Jews, both religious and non-religious, strongly oppose Zionist practice, arguing that Jewish identity is not compatible with the dispossession of Palestinians. These Jews advocate for a future in which Palestinians and Israeli Jews might live together on the land in a relationship of equality and justice.

What is Christian Zionism? What do Christians believe about Zionism?

Some Christians are Zionists. They believe that it is part of God's plan to establish a Jewish state in Palestine. Christian Zionists believe that God's promise of the land to the Jewish people means that they must support the State of Israel. For some Christians, support of Zionism serves as a form of repentance for Western Christianity's shameful history of anti-Judaism. For other Christians, specifically those who read the Bible through the lens of a theology known as dispensationalism, support of Zionism is motivated by the belief that the creation of the State of Israel is an essential step on the way to Jesus' Second Coming. Although dispensationalists are strong supporters of Israel, their theological approach has an anti-Jewish bias. According to this theology, at the time of Jesus' Second Coming most Jews will be eternally condemned to hell. Palestinian Christians, many of whom have suffered tremendously at the hands of the State of Israel, find it hard to understand why some Western Christians support Zionism. Christians in other Middle Eastern countries find this support equally puzzling. Uncritical Western Christian support of Zionism hampers the witness of the church in the Middle East; it causes some Muslims to associate Middle Eastern Christians and Christianity in general with the pro-Zionist beliefs of Western Christian Zionists. Christians in Palestine and the rest of the Middle East argue that the Bible, which testifies to God incarnate in Jesus Christ, should not be used to justify the confiscation of Palestinian land, the destruction of Palestinian homes, violations of Palestinian human rights and the denial of justice to Palestinian refugees.

Didn't God give the land to the Jews?

How should Christians understand biblical promises of the land to Abraham and his descendants? (See, for example, Genesis 15:18-21 and Genesis 17:7-9.) One way to approach this question is to ask, "Who are the descendants of Abraham?" The Apostle Paul would answer that "he is the father of all of us," that God's promises to Abraham are for all of his descendants, "not only to the adherents of the law but

also to those who share the faith of Abraham" (Romans 4:16). God's promise of the land to Abraham and his descendants, then, should not be seen as a warrant for exclusive Israeli Jewish control over the land today, but rather suggests that the land is a place for all those— Jewish, Christian and Muslim—who claim Abraham as their father. The land is not the exclusive possession of one people, but can embrace Jews and Gentiles, both Israeli Jews and Palestinians.

Another way to approach the question is to think about the conditions of God's gift of land. Scripture repeatedly warns that failure to live righteously means jeopardizing the gift of land: "You shall keep all my statutes and all my ordinances, and observe them," Leviticus stresses, "so that the land to which I bring you to settle in may not vomit you out" (Leviticus 20:22). Many Israelis critical of their government's military rule in the West Bank and the Gaza Strip poignantly suggest that Israel fails to keep God's statues and ordinances when it occupies another people and violates their human rights on a daily basis. The biblical prophets were also critical of the unjust acquisition of land. Elijah is blunt in his message to King Ahab after Ahab takes over Naboth's vineyard: "Thus says the LORD: Have you killed, and also taken possession?" (1 Kings 21:19). Yet the State of Israel "took possession" of the

A bullet-riddled Qur'an was one of the few items that survived the rocket attack on Sami Jubrin's home.

homes and properties of the Palestinians who fled or whom it expelled during the fighting of 1948, forbidding them to return, and today it takes possession of land from Palestinian farmers in order to build settlements, bypass roads, and its separation barrier in the Occupied Territories.

A third approach to the question of the promise of land is to remember that ultimately it is God, not individuals or nations, who owns the land. "The land is mine," God proclaims, "with me you are but aliens and tenants" (Leviticus 25:23). God issues this reminder to the people of Israel in the course of instituting the Jubilee, the acceptable year of the Lord. Jesus, in his inaugural sermon in Nazareth (Luke 4), has the audacity to declare the acceptable year of the Lord, with its Jubilee promises of justice in the land. A people that remembers its alien status in the land will not dispossess others and treat them as aliens. God's promise of the land therefore cannot mean the dispossession of Palestinians, the destruction of their homes, and the confiscation of their land.

The Rev. Naim Ateek, a prominent Palestinian Christian theologian, observes that the concepts of peace and justice are intertwined in the Old Testament. The Hebrew word "shalom" and the Arabic world "salaam" share the same linguistic root and point to a common concept of peace, justice, wholeness, health and security. Peace, Ateek insists, cannot be achieved without justice, a reality illustrated by the prophet Isaiah: "Then justice will dwell in the wilderness and righteousness abide in the fruitful field. And the effect of righteousness will be peace, and the result of righteousness, quietness and trust forever" (Isaiah 32:16-17).

Aren't we as Christians supposed to "bless Israel"?

Some Christians hesitate to criticize Israeli military policies, citing the biblical injunction to "bless Israel." While Scripture does not actually talk about "blessing Israel," God does promise Abraham that "I will bless those who bless you, and the one who curses you I will curse; and in you all the families of the earth shall be blessed" (Genesis 12:3). Even if we read this promise to Abraham as applying only to the Jewish people, we must still ask ourselves what it means to "bless" the Jewish people and the State of Israel today. Is it to give uncritical and unconditional support to Israel? Or does blessing Israel instead mean calling upon Israel to love mercy and do justice in the land?

Is criticism of Israel anti-Jewish?

Supporters of justice, peace and reconciliation condemn all forms of anti-Judaism. (The term "anti-Judaism" is preferable to the more common term "anti-Semitism." Anti-Semitism technically refers to discrimination against all Semitic peoples, a category that includes Arabs as well as Jews.) Critiquing discriminatory and oppressive policies carried out by the State of Israel is not anti-Jewish; many Jews themselves criticize Israel's destructive policies, arguing that house demolitions, land confiscations, and disproportionate use of lethal force are not compatible with Jewish practice and belief. Christian critiques of Israeli policies should be made in a spirit of humility and should not use anti-Jewish stereotypes when describing the oppressive Israeli practices in the Occupied Territories.

Are there religious visions for justice and peace in Palestine-Israel?

While religion fuels political visions and ideologies of conquest, violence and revenge, it also energizes those working for peace, justice and reconciliation. Every day, Mennonite workers in Palestine-Israel meet Muslims, Christians, and Jews, both regular people and community leaders, who are committed to their religious traditions and who yearn for a future of peace with justice. At the Sabeel Ecumenical Liberation Theology Center, Palestinian Christians promote nonviolence and work alongside Palestinian Muslims and Israeli Jews for freedom and equality. Rabbis for Human Rights, an Israeli Jewish organization, works for the renewal (tikkun) of the world by engaging in such acts as helping Palestinians harvest olives when they are threatened by Israeli settlers. Palestinian Muslims associated with a Mennonite Central Committee partner organization like the Culture and Free Thought Association in the Khan Younis refugee camp live and work as committed Muslims who strive for peace, justice and reconciliation.

Im Munir, the matriarch of the Odeh family sits on the couch on the Odeh home.

Conflict & Hope

A tree is decorated with the faces of people killed in the violence in the Gaza Strip at the Bunat Lalghad (center for teens) in the Gaza Strip.

5. Continuing Conflict, Sources of Hope

What is terrorism? What about suicide bombings?

Terrorism is typically defined as violence against civilians in service of a political cause. One of the most visible forms of terrorism in the Israel-Palestine conflict is the practice of suicide bombings. As the phenomenon appears in Palestine-Israel, the bombings are carried out by Palestinians who strap explosives to their bodies and then detonate themselves in the presence of Israeli soldiers or civilians, killing themselves and usually a number of people around them. The bombers are often young men, but young women and older men have also perpetrated such attacks.

What are North American Christians to make of such disturbing actions? Certainly, as we look at newspaper photos of an empty baby stroller standing in the debris left after an attack, or hear of cell phones ringing in the wreckage of a blown-up bus, never to be answered again, our hearts go out to the victims. There is no possible justification for such horrible crimes.

As Christians committed to spreading the good news of Christ's kingdom, including his message of justice and peace for all people, Mennonite workers categorically condemn suicide bombings. Mennonites, as Christians committed to nonviolent peacemaking, oppose all forms of violence. While Christians can recognize the despair that many Palestinians living through occupation feel, we must deplore suicide bombings, along with all forms of violence in Palestine-Israel, mourning the senseless loss of life.

The majority of ordinary Palestinians oppose the killing of Israeli civilians. Certainly the official Palestinian leadership, including former President Yassir Arafat and current Palestinian leader Mahmoud Abbas (Abu Mazen), have consistently condemned suicide bombings and to the extent possible tried to prevent them from occurring. These Palestinian leaders know that suicide bombings destroy their credibility and severely limit hopes for a peaceful resolution to the conflict.

Christians can try to understand and to explain the reality that produces suicide bombers, but never to excuse or justify the practice. Some Palestinians say that the brutal conditions, endless frustration, and forced hopelessness of the Israeli occupation lead many young people to believe that the best contribution they can make is to "sacrifice" their life for their country. As one Palestinian mechanic put it while waiting hours at an Israeli checkpoint on his way to work: "I know this from my work as a mechanic. If pressure is applied at some point, it must be released at another. This process explains the rise of the suicide bombers."

While many Palestinians deplore violent actions that target civilians, they also ask why the deaths of Palestinian civilians are not given equal weight. When scores of Palestinian civilians are killed as "collateral damage" during Israeli assassination attempts on wanted men, when children on their way to school in Khan Younis are killed by a bomb left on the side of the road, when an elderly woman in Nablus is killed by a seemingly random shooting, Palestinians wonder why the world does not label these actions as "terrorism." Palestinians also observe that much of Israel's military hardware comes from the United States and ruefully ask why the United States does not object when its F-16 fighter planes and Apache helicopters are used in military actions that result in civilian deaths and injuries.

What are the continuing sources of conflict?

The Oslo process deferred five issues to "final status" negotiations. These five issues continue to be at the heart of the ongoing Palestinian-Israeli conflict.

Settlements: Israel continues to build settlements, or colonies, in the Occupied Territories. Illegal under international law, these Israeli colonies take over Palestinian land and break up connections between Palestinian cities and villages. Thanks to settlements and bypass roads connecting the settlements, travel for Palestinians within the West Bank becomes difficult to impossible. Jerusalem, meanwhile, has been progressively cut off from the rest of the West Bank by settlements and bypass

roads. Today there are nearly 430,000 Israeli settlers (including those in East Jerusalem) in nearly 200 illegal Israeli settlements and around 100 settler outposts. The separation barrier being built throughout the West Bank is a dramatic extension of the settlement enterprise, as it de facto annexes many settlements into Israel proper while leaving Palestinians in disconnected enclaves.

Water: The Palestinian Hydrology Group records that 75 percent of the renewable water resources in the West Bank and the Gaza Strip are used by Israel, both for settlements and for use inside Israel proper. While Israel confiscates water resources from the Occupied Territories, nearly 200,000 Palestinians do not enjoy running water. The path of the separation barrier in the northern West Bank, meanwhile, solidifies Israeli control over Palestinian groundwater aquifers.

Jerusalem: Palestinians want East Jerusalem, including the Muslim, Armenian and Christian quarters of the Old City, as their capital. The State of Israel, however, wants exclusive sovereignty over all of the city; through colonization and the construction of the separation barrier, it is cutting Jerusalem off from nearby West Bank villages and cities. Some Israelis insist that Palestinians must recognize Israeli rights on the Temple Mount/Haram al-Sharif if there is to be peace. Other Israelis, however, argue that the rebuilding of the Temple will be the work of the Messiah: Israelis, they argue, should not insist on sovereignty over the Temple Mount if doing so would scuttle a chance for peace and reconciliation.

Refugees: Palestinians insist that any durable peace must include an Israeli recognition of the rights of Palestinian refugees to return and compensation, rights upheld by the United Nations (UN General Assembly resolution 194) and in international law. The majority of Israelis, however, categorically rejects the return of Palestinian refugees, fearing that refugee return would endanger the Jewish demographic majority within Israel and thus endanger its identity as a Jewish state. Some Israelis, however, consider a frank discussion of the Palestinian refugee crisis to be an integral part of durable peace-building. For example, the Zochrot Association, an Israeli Jewish initiative, promotes dialogue within Israeli society about Palestinian refugee rights by "remembering the Nakba in Hebrew." Zochrot was one of Mennonite Central Committee's first Israeli partners, and was the first organization to support Zochrot financially.

Borders: Palestinians who endorse a two-state solution to the Palestinian-Israeli conflict insist that the borders of the Palestinian state must correspond with the demarcation lines of June 4, 1967. In other words, the Palestinian state must comprise all of the Occupied Territories of East Jerusalem, the West Bank and the Gaza Strip. Some Palestinians have discussed potential adjustments to these borders in a final settlement with Israel, as long as the Palestinian state received land from inside Israel equivalent in size and quality to compensate for any changes to the Green Line. Israeli proposals, however, have involved creating autonomous Palestinian

areas or "statelets" in anywhere between 40 to 80 percent of the Occupied Territories.

What are possible solutions to the Palestinian-Israeli conflict?

Mennonite workers in Palestine-Israel are often asked what they see as the solution to the conflict in Palestine-Israel. Mennonite organizations don't officially advocate for any particular global political solution to this complex problem. Instead, Mennonites support a framework which will allow Palestinians and Israelis to enjoy the "secure dwellings" of (Isaiah 32:18), to sit securely under vine and fig tree (Micah 4:4). International law, with its prohibitions of illegal confiscation of land and other natural resources, its provisions for the return and compensation of refugees, and its curbs on violence, all are important elements of any political solution that seeks to secure "secure dwellings" for Palestinians and Israelis. Some Palestinians and Israelis believe that justice, peace, and secure dwellings can best be achieved through a "two-state solution" to the conflict, while other Israelis and Palestinians suggest that this vision is most compatible with the establishment of one bi-national state in which Palestinians and Israelis would be equal citizens. Any proposed resolution to the Palestinian-Israeli conflict (for example, the Bush administration's

Road Map) must be judged as to whether or not it provides secure dwellings by ending the occupation, reversing the legitimization of land confiscation and colonization, and allowing for the return and compensation of Palestinian refugees. The current Israeli policy of "convergence" and "unilateral separation," unfortunately, fails to provide secure dwellings, instead solidifying the occupation and Palestinian dispossession.

What is the "one-state" solution?

When people talk about final resolutions to the Palestine-Israel conflict they often refer to two basic options, known as the "one-state" solution and the "two-state" solution. The one-state solution means that all of the territory now making up Israel proper, the West Bank and the Gaza Strip would be united into a single country. This "one-state" would be a bi-national state, which means that it would be home to two peoples, the Israelis and the Palestinians. Instead of a Jewish state (as Israel is now) or a Muslim state (as a minority of Palestinians hope an independent Palestine would be), the newly created binational state would be a secular state with equal rights for all of its citizens.

What is the "two-state" solution?

The two-state solution involves creating two separate independent states, the State of Israel for Jews and the State of Palestine for Palestinians. Under the two-state solution, Israel would end its occupation of the West Bank and Gaza Strip and withdraw from part or all of this territory. The Palestinians would then form an independent state of Palestine on the remaining land in the West Bank and Gaza Strip. How much of the West Bank and Gaza Strip would be offered to the Palestinians for the creation of their state is one of the major controversies of the conflict. Palestinians insist that, if the two-state solution is to be economically viable for Palestinians and is to meet the minimum demands of justice, the Palestinian state must comprise all of the West Bank, East Jerusalem, and the Gaza Strip (22 percent of Mandate Palestine). The ongoing Israeli colonization of the Occupied Territories, however, is making the implementation of such a solution increasingly difficult.

What are the advantages and disadvantages of these solutions? Is a two-state solution still possible?

The one-state solution features several distinct advantages. Having one state would allow Palestinian refugees to return to their original homes. In contrast, under many versions of the two-state solution discussed by Palestinians, Israelis and international mediators, Palestinian refugees would be repatriated to the new state of Palestine but would not be allowed to return to their original homes in what is now Israel. The two-state solution, furthermore, does not address the systematic discrimination faced by Palestinian Christians and Muslims inside Israel.

Proponents of the two-state solution, including the Israelis who favor this outcome, argue that it is pragmatic and realistic. While it might not meet the demands of justice, they say, it is the best to which Palestinians can aspire while simultaneously meeting the need for Israeli security. Other Israelis believe that even a two-state solution is incompatible with Israeli security; they fear that a Palestinian state would inevitably be hostile to Israel and put Israelis at risk. For these Israelis, security means no more than quasi-autonomy for Palestinians. Other Palestinians and Israelis suggest that ethnically-based states are anachronisms: rather than working for a "Jewish state" or a "Palestinian state," persons concerned with justice and reconciliation should strive for futures in which national boundaries are transcended. Regardless of whether one favors a two-state or a one-state solution to the conflict, facts on the ground are rapidly undermining the possibility of a two-state solution. Israeli colonies around Jerusalem, Bethlehem, Hebron, and in the northern West Bank are making any future contiguous

Neama Mahmod Harb pulls bits of clothing from a bag. The clothes were wore by her sister Azaza and friend Rahma Shahean who were accidentally killed when Israeli helicopters launched rockets at a car during the political assassination of Hosan Awbait.

Palestinian state impossible. Many Palestinians and Israelis fear that the separation barrier, the latest stage of Israeli colonization, is the final nail in the coffin of a two-state solution, as it is creating de facto political borders, leaving Palestinians with at most 40 percent of the West Bank, with no connection to Jerusalem.

What does the future hold for Palestine and Israel if the one-state or two-state solutions are not implemented?

If the difficulties of the one-state or two-state solutions cannot be overcome, the future of Palestine-Israel looks very bleak indeed. One of the few principles that all parties in the conflict can agree on is that the status quo cannot continue; the levels of violence and human suffering are too high to make the current arrangements a sustainable or desirable option. Unfortunately the other probable scenarios, known as "unilateral separation"/"convergence" and "transfer," are equally discouraging. In the first scenario, Israel continues implementing its policy of unilateral separation. This involves maintaining control over the Occupied Territories while enclosing Palestinians—through the separation barrier, with its eight-meter concrete walls and electronic fences, and through trenches, barbed wire, checkpoints and military roadblocks—into ever smaller pieces of territory. The separation barrier is the most visible manifestation of this plan. Unilateral separation might eventually produce a climate in which Palestinians would be allowed to call their disconnected territorial islands a "state," but such a designation would only disguise, not alter, the reality of turning Palestinian cities into economically dependent reservations. This strategy of "unilateral separation" allows Israel to have its cake and eat it too: Israel remains in full control of the West Bank and Gaza Strip while simultaneously creating the illusion that the occupation has ended. More and more Palestinians, Israelis and international observers are calling unilateral separation a form of apartheid.

The second scenario, known as "transfer," is even more troubling. In Israeli political discourse, "transfer" is a euphemism for another euphemism: "ethnic cleansing." Right-wing Israeli parties, including some which have participated in coalition governments, call for the "transfer" of Palestinians out of the Occupied Territories in order to create a Palestinian-free space.

Response

Students at an MCC-sponsored kindergarten in the West Bank village of Deir Ibziya.

6. How Mennonites are Responding, How You Can Help

Which Mennonite agencies are working in Palestine-Israel?

Mennonite-related organizations working in Palestine-Israel include:

Mennonite Central Committee (MCC), a relief, development, and peacebuilding organization of Mennonite and Brethren in Christian churches in Canada and the United States;

Mission Network, the mission agency of Mennonite Church USA, and Mennonite Church Canada Witness;

Eastern Mennonite Missions, the mission agency of the Lancaster Mennonite Conference; and Christian Peacemaker Teams.

What do the Mennonite mission agencies do in Palestine-Israel?

Mennonite Mission Network (MMN, formerly Mennonite Board of Missions and Commission on Overseas Missions) has been involved in Israel since 1953 when the first workers arrived in the country. Working mainly with Messianic Jewish communities, these Mennonites were involved in leadership training, ecumenical cooperation, interfaith dialogue, tourism and publication businesses, student evangelism, and congregational pastoral roles. Some early energy went into the development of a "Christian Moshav (agricultural community)" called Nes Ammim in Galilee. In the 1960s Mennonite workers began medical work at the Nazareth Hospital, where workers served in many capacities, culminating in the establishment of a nursing school. MMN has also provided support to the Mar Elias Educational Institutions in Ibillin, spearheaded by Archbishop Elias Chacour. In recent years, MMN has focused attention on three general areas of ministry. First, long-term work with the Messianic Jewish community continues, with special emphasis on pastoral training and Jewish evangelism. Second, Mennonites and especially long-term Mennonite workers have helped envision and establish Nazareth Village, a re-creation of a first-century Jewish village, where the cultural environment that nurtured Jesus can be shared with local Jewish, Christian, and Muslim visitors, along with international tourists. Third, Mennonite workers based in Jerusalem have maintained interfaith connections, organized and resourced tour groups visiting Palestine-Israel, and produced publications to help North Americans and other Christians better understand the biblical, historical, and current political realities of the region. Mennonite Church Canada Witness collaborates with MMN on much of its work in Palestine-Israel. Workers with Eastern Mennonite Missions, meanwhile, help support churches and networks of Messianic Jewish believers inside Israel.

What does Christian Peacemaker Teams do in Palestine-Israel?

At the invitation of the Hebron municipality, Christian Peacemaker Teams (CPT) maintains a year-round presence in the heart of the old city of Hebron in the southern West Bank. CPT volunteers seek to be a violence-reducing presence in the midst of this tension-filled city. They accompany Palestinian children to school in order to protect them from harassment from Israeli settlers, protest house demolitions, and highlight harsh conditions facing Palestinians living in Hebron's old city. CPT routinely works in partnership with Israeli organizations such as Israeli Committee Against House Demolitions and Rabbis for Human Rights.

CPT workers have highlighted the impact of Israeli settlements on average Palestinians in other parts of the West Bank, particularly the effect of land confiscations and house demolitions. Recently, CPT has had a team of workers in the southern West Bank village of al-Tuwani, whose livelihood and future, like that of other southern West Bank villages, are threatened by the construction of the separation barrier. CPT workers in al-Tuwani also accompany Palestinian children to school who have been regularly harassed by Israeli settlers.

What brought MCC to work with Palestinians?

MCC has worked in Palestine for nearly sixty years. Arriving in 1949 to provide material assistance to Palestinian refugees driven from their homes in the War of

1948, MCC stayed to work alongside Palestinians in their search for justice, peace and freedom. Through Christian education, peacebuilding, the promotion of Palestinian needlework, and rural development, MCC has supported vital initiatives to strengthen Palestinian society. In the six-decade history of MCC Palestine, nearly 200 North American service workers have volunteered in the program.

MCC was moved by the plight of Palestinian refugees from the War of 1948 to begin work in Palestine. In the early years many MCC workers provided material aid to refugees. Numerous Christmas bundles, containing much-appreciated clothing, were distributed, along with MCC canned meat, comforters and layettes. MCC also worked hard to empower refugees to help themselves. In the West Bank, early MCC workers started sewing programs for refugee women and shoemaking and carpentry programs for refugee men.

In the early 1950s, MCC began a groundbreaking Palestinian needlework program. The program worked with up to 500 women at any given time in villages around Bethlehem and Hebron and in the refugee camps of Jericho. These needlework pieces were some of the first items in the nascent SELF-HELP Crafts enterprise, today Ten Thousand Villages.

For many years, MCC was also known in the Palestinian community for its support of Palestinian Christian schools serving both Christian and Muslim students. The Arab Evangelical Orphanage in Hebron, the Hope Secondary School in Beit Jala, and the Latin Patriarchate School in Zababdeh have all enjoyed the contributions of MCC service workers and have been supported financially by MCC. From the mid-1970s to the mid-1980s, MCC's rural development unit worked with thousands of Palestinian farmers as they introduced drip irrigation networks, reclaimed land for cultivation, and planted tens of thousands of fruit trees. As the Israeli military authorities routinely looked to confiscate uncultivated land, MCC's work in rural development had a markedly political character.

Gradually, as the capacities of the local Palestinian population developed, MCC began to turn its projects over to Palestinian administration. The role of MCC in Palestine became one of catalyst and supporter of Palestinian initiatives. MCC support of the Palestinian Center for Rapprochement between Peoples exemplified this type of support in which MCC assisted Palestinian Christians in Beit Sahour as they created a movement to initiate grassroots dialogue with Israelis and to promote nonviolent resistance to the occupation. MCC also began entering into partnerships with local Palestinian organizations in fields such as agriculture, women's development and the rehabilitation of persons with disabilities. These relationships provided an opportunity for MCC to learn from local people as well as to assist local groups with grants, loans, training, and other needs.

As time passed, MCC workers began to see the problems in Palestine less as requiring emergency material assistance or capacity building and more as requiring justice and peacebuilding. Sustainable economic development, it became clear, could not happen under the harsh conditions of occupation. In the 1980s MCC began to assign North American peace development workers to serve in partnership with Palestinian peacemaking initiatives. By the summer of 2002, Palestinian non-governmental organizations (NGOs) had become unable to carry out their work due to increasing Israeli restrictions on freedom of movement and Israel's occupation policies that made normal life impossible. In this context, MCC workers redoubled their efforts to communicate with MCC constituents in North America about the dire situation facing Palestinians and Israelis.

What is the focus of MCC's work in the Occupied Territories today?

MCC's work in Palestine today has two areas of emphasis: supporting the witness of the local Palestinian churches and working with Palestinian and Israeli groups pursuing justice and peace. MCC supports dynamic projects carried out by a variety of church-related and grassroots organizations, including:

- The Wi'am Conflict Resolution Center in Bethlehem, modeling nonviolent conflict transformation within Palestinian society.

- The Sabeel Ecumenical Liberation Theology Center, providing a theological and spiritual resource for the Palestinian church.

- The Badil Refugee Resource Center, researching and advocating for durable solutions for Palestinian refugees.

- The YMCA Rehabilitation Program, working with Palestinians with disabilities, including those injured by the Israeli military.

- The Zochrot Association, an Israeli organization dedicated to raising Israeli awareness about Palestinian refugees by "remembering the Nakba in Hebrew."

- The YMCA Women's Training Program, supporting sustainable economic development.

- The Culture and Free Thought Association in the Khan Yunis refugee camp in the Gaza Strip, providing creative learning opportunities and psychosocial services for children and teenagers with the support of MCC's Global Family sponsorship program.

- The Latin (Roman Catholic) Patriarchate School in Zababdeh: MCC's Global Family sponsorship program provides scholarships for Christian students whose families find it difficult to pay the minimal school fees. North American service workers are seconded to the school to work in English language teaching and community development.

Does MCC "take sides" with Palestinians and against Israelis?

As a Christian organization, MCC does not "take sides" for Palestinians and against Israelis, knowing that both Palestinians and Israelis are children of God made in God's image. MCC workers do not "take sides" in prayer, but rather petition God that Israelis and Palestinians alike might dwell in God's peace. MCC does "take sides" with the good news of Christ that reconciliation between enemies is possible and that reconciliation involves the doing of justice. MCC does "take sides" against all forms of violence, regardless of who perpetrates it. MCC also "takes sides" against a false neutrality that portrays Palestinians and Israelis as equal parties to the conflict and that avoids the task of identifying military occupation, siege and dispossession as injustice. Finally, MCC "takes sides" with courageous Israeli peace groups and nonviolent Palestinian groups who struggle jointly against military occupation and through that struggle form new bonds of solidarity and cooperation. Please pray that Mennonite workers in Palestine-Israel might have wisdom, love, courage and strength as they seek to discern how and when to "take sides."

Does MCC work with Israelis?

Yes, MCC works with Israelis in several different ways. MCC's peace development workers regularly meet and consult with members of Israeli peacebuilding organizations such as Ta'ayush (a joint Palestinian-Israeli initiative whose name means "coexistence"), Gush Shalom (the Israeli peace bloc) and Rabbis for Human Rights. MCC also provides support to Israeli peacebuilding initiatives such as the Israeli Committee against House Demolitions, devoted to protesting the destruction of Palestinian homes, and Zochrot, an Israeli organization committed to raising awareness of the events of 1948 and to making a just resolution of the Palestinian refugee crisis the foundation of future Palestinian-Israeli peace and reconciliation.

Suha Namrwouty (6, grade 1) learns letters and sounds from Ifidal Abu Madil at the Sharouq u Amal (Sunrise and Hope) children's center, Khan Younis, Gaza.

Why does MCC work with Muslims?

MCC works with Muslims for two main reasons. First, Muslims make up about 98 percent of the Palestinian population. In this context it is natural for an organization like MCC, which emphasizes the importance of personal relationships, to be involved with Muslims on a daily basis. MCC workers relate to Muslims in a variety of settings. They have Muslims as students and teachers, friends and neighbors, employees and colleagues.

MCC also works with Muslims in Palestine as a way of witnessing to the possibility of peace between peoples of different religions. In Palestine-Israel there are many examples of fear, hatred and mistrust based on religion. In one way or another Christians, Muslims and Jews all deal with the negative consequences of religious prejudice every day. In this context, MCC Palestine believes that working with Palestinian Muslims as well as Christians is an important part of witnessing to the right relationships between people that characterize the Kingdom of God.

Why are there no Mennonite churches in the Middle East?

When Mennonites first came to work in the Middle East, a conscious decision was made not to plant Mennonite churches but rather to support the local churches already present in the region. When the first Mennonite workers came to Palestine in 1949, ten to fifteen percent of the local Palestinian population was Christian. The majority of these Christians were Greek Orthodox. Some were also Roman Catholics or Greek Catholics (also known as Melkites). A minority were Protestants, including small numbers of Baptists, Lutherans, and Anglicans. North American Mennonites believed it was more important to support these local churches than to compete with them by introducing yet another denomination. There was already some resentment in the local Christian community regarding "sheep stealing," the

In Qalqiliya, West Bank, Makedi Silmi picks cucumbers on a farm that is part of an MCC-sponsored irrigation project. Limited water resources in the occupied West Bank are made even scarcer by Israeli confiscation of water from West Bank aquifers. MCC projects help Palestinian farmers renovate old and broken irrigation networks, some of which were damaged during the construction of the Israeli separation barrier.

practice of drawing Christians from one denomination to another. Instead of planting Mennonite churches, Mennonites began to work with all sectors of the Christian community.

Inside Israel, the Mennonite mission agencies work in partnership with Palestinian Christian churches and institutions together with Messianic Jewish congregations, walking alongside them in their ministries and outreach.

The practice of not planting Mennonite churches in the Middle East is sometimes questioned by North American Mennonites. Middle Eastern Christians, however, consistently report that this policy is one of the things they most appreciate about Mennonites. Mennonite workers do share their Mennonite beliefs with their Palestinian and Israeli brothers and sisters. Together with the local churches, they strive to promote Mennonite values like

peacebuilding, following Jesus and having a personal relationship with God. These values are also held by many local Christians. Mennonite experience in Palestine-Israel belies the belief that the Eastern Church is spiritually dead. Many Palestinian Christians find within the Orthodox, Catholic, or Protestant faiths a deep well of spirituality that sustains them as a minority religion living under Israeli occupation. Palestinian Christians, moreover, have been at the forefront of the Palestinian nonviolent movement and in the struggle for justice, peace, and reconciliation.

What sustains Mennonite work in Palestine-Israel?

Mennonite workers in Palestine-Israel are sustained by their faith in God who conquered the powers of sin and death through Jesus Christ and who raises up witnesses for justice, peace and reconciliation through the Holy Spirit. Although Mennonite workers sometimes become discouraged, they are rejuvenated when they see God's reconciling Spirit at work, bringing Palestinians and Israelis together to rebuild a Palestinian home destroyed by Israeli military bulldozers; when they work with Palestinians, Christians and Muslims, engaged in nonviolent protests against military occupation; and when they worship alongside Christians from Palestine-Israel.

What can we do?

How can North American Christians respond to the tragic situation in Palestine-Israel? What is the role of Mennonites, as believers in the nonviolent Gospel of Jesus Christ, in this conflict? How do we live with the knowledge that United States' tax dollars pay for bullets used by the Israeli army, Apache helicopters attacking Palestinian towns, and F-16s that terrorize Palestinian cities? What risks should North American Mennonites be willing to take to promote justice and peace in the Middle East?

Pray: To receive frequent prayer requests on the situation in Palestine-Israel, send your e-mail address to pwopt@ mennonitecc.ca. Some sample prayers from Mennonite workers in Palestine-Israel:

Pray that Mennonite workers in the occupied Palestinian territories might be granted the wisdom to know when and how to "take sides." Pray for Mennonite workers in Palestine-Israel, that they might live and witness in word and deed to the reconciling love of God made manifest in Jesus Christ.

Pray for the church in Palestine-Israel, that its witness might be sustained and strengthened.

Pray for Palestinians opposing violence in the resistance to Israeli occupation.

Pray for conscientious objectors in Israel who refuse to serve in the Israeli army.

Pray for Israeli soldiers who refuse to serve in the Occupied Territories.

Pray for children in Palestine-Israel: Pray for Palestinian children, who live daily with the threat of violence and arbitrary killing, who see Israeli soldiers with guns and tanks patrolling their streets, who spend too many days of their childhood in their houses under military curfew, unable to go out and play, knowing that even stepping onto the porch or balcony could draw Israeli gunfire. Remember them in your prayers as they wait for hours at checkpoints, watching their parents and grandparents humiliated by teenage Israeli soldiers, kept away from school, church, mosque, and medical care by Israeli policies of collective punishment. Pray that God grant them some joys of childhood despite these difficult conditions, and to keep their hearts free of hate and full of hope for a just and peaceful settlement. Pray for Israeli children, who live in fear of suicide bombers on buses and in stores. Pray that they might not grow up with hate in their hearts. Pray for young Israeli men and women required to do military service, and pray for strength for those who refuse to serve for reasons of conscience.

Share: Contribute time or money to Mennonite organizations working in Palestine-Israel or specifically to their Palestine-Israel programs. The MCC web site (www.mcc.org) has examples of giving projects suitable for families, Sunday school classes, and congregations. MCC's Global Family program is a good place to start. In Palestine, Global Family supports Christian education in the West Bank town of Zababdeh and psychosocial programs for children in Gaza through the Culture and Free Thought Association. Visit the web sites of Mennnonite Mission Network, Christian Peacemaker Teams, and Eastern Mennonite Missions for ideas on how to support their ministries.

Advocate: Work to change United States foreign policy in the Middle East. Raise awareness in your church and community of issues of peace and justice in Palestine-Israel. If you are from the United States, ask that your tax dollars not go to support the Israeli occupation.

Stay informed: MCC workers send monthly e-mail updates on MCC's work in Palestine-Israel. To receive these updates, send your e-mail address to pwopt@ mennonitecc.ca.

U.S. citizens can subscribe to the MCC Washington Memo and act on "Action Alerts" sent out by the MCC Washington Office. (For more information, visit mcc.org/us/washington.) Follow news of the conflict, but remember that the North American mainstream media does not tell the whole story. Seek out alternative sources of information such as the periodicals, books and web sites mentioned in the final section of this booklet.

Learn more about MCC's work in Palestine on the MCC web site (mcc.org). The web site includes service opportunities, news stories, photos, articles, program updates, giving projects, worship resources, prayer requests and more. You are also invited to check out the resources for further study listed in the Resources section.

Meet a Palestinian Peacebuilder: Nora Carmi, Sabeel

"Remember that Christianity started here and that I am a descendant of the continuous non-stopping witness of Christianity in this land," urges Nora Carmi, director of local programs at the Sabeel Ecumenical Liberation Theology Center. "Christianity was not imported . . . to this land. And we are the few faithful remnants who are living and witnessing every single day." Nora organizes theological and spiritual workshops for Palestinian Christian clergy, lay people, and women's and youth groups, seeking to support and strengthen the Palestinian Christian witness for the gospel and its message of peace, justice, and reconciliation. Nora takes inspiration in her work from Jesus' example. "For us Palestinian Christians there is a lot we can learn from our model, Jesus Christ," she shares. "How did Christ resist the occupation? What can we learn from Christ in our resistance? How can we resist with dignity, respect, nonviolently but yet have the courage to speak out, because we cannot remain silent when there is injustice."

Meet a Palestinian Peacebuilder: Zoughbi Zoughbi, Wi'am

"The reality of our life is living trapped by fear," says Zoughbi Zoughbi, director of the Wi'am Center for Conflict Resolution in Bethlehem. Economic insecurity, restrictions on movement and the possibility of military invasion all contribute to Palestinians' fears, according to Zoughbi. The Wi'am Center mediates conflicts among Palestinians and trains educators to work with children living through traumatic events. Zoughbi and his co-workers "try to help people address injustice rather than avenge it." Palestinian Christians, Zoughbi believes, are "Christians of the cross, awaiting resurrection." Security, he continues, will not come through vengeance, but through a future of peace and justice for Palestinians and Israelis alike. "We need to bring Israel to its senses, not to its knees," he says.

Meet a Palestinian Peacebuilder: Amal Khoudeir, Culture and Free Thought Association

"The children here are older than they should be," says Amal Khoudeir, director of the Bunat al-Ghad (Builders of the Future) center for teenagers in the Khan Younis refugee camp in the southern Gaza Strip. "They've seen too much, grown up too fast." A devout Muslim woman, Khoudeir is committed to providing Palestinian children and teenagers with safe spaces to develop their intellects and creativity and to empowering Palestinian girls. In the summer of 2000, Amal attended the Summer Peacebuilding Institute at Eastern Mennonite University, where she was reinforced in her conviction that peace without justice cannot last. For Amal, the biggest challenge in her work is to provide children with a sense of hope amidst routine military invasions. "How can we inspire them, give them hope?" she asks. "That is our task."

Meet an Israeli Peacebuilder: Eitan Bronstein, Zochrot

The father of four children, Eitan Bronstein directs the Zochrot Association, an Israeli initiative to promote discussion of the Palestinian Nakba of 1948 within Israeli society. Zochrot organizes visits by Israelis to the sites of destroyed Palestinian villages, where they hear from refugees about the history of the village and how its residents were expelled. Zochrot then places signs in Hebrew and Arabic at the site, bringing an erased past momentarily back to life. "I believe that the right of return [for Palestinian refugees] is a condition for reconciliation," Bronstein says. Bronstein challenges the students with whom he works to learn about the erased history of the countryside, starting with "Canada Park" near the School for Peace. This national park planted with trees donated by the Canadian Jewish community is built on the site of three Palestinian villages (Imwas, Yalu, and Beit Nuba) destroyed in 1967. "Students often resist hearing about the past, and when they don't deny the past, they often want to justify it. Education is a long, hard process."

Meet an Israeli Peacebuilder: Jeff Halper, Israeli Committee Against House Demolitions

For Jeff Halper, a teacher of sociology at the Hebrew University in Jerusalem, stopping Israeli demolition of Palestinian homes is about promoting reconciliation. House demolitions, he observes, have been "at the center of the Israeli struggle against the Palestinians" since 1948. The "message" sent by Israeli bulldozers, according to Halper, is that "You [the Palestinians] do not belong here. We uprooted you from your homes in 1948 and now we will uproot you from all of the Land of Israel." Halper and his colleagues at the Israeli Committee Against House Demolitions (ICAHD) believe that the way of peace, justice and reconciliation takes a different route than that of the bulldozer. In addition to raising awareness within Israel and internationally about house demolitions, ICAHD staff join with Palestinians to rebuild destroyed Palestinian homes, building peace from the ground up.

Ismail Mohammed Khudeir (foreground) and fellow fisherman haul their nets from the Mediterranean Sea on the Gaza coast.

Resources

A student at the Dar Al-Luiqman Kindergarten in the Khan Younis Refugee Camp of the Gaza Strip.

7. Resources for Further Study

A. Mennonite Materials

Books

Hebron Journal: Stories of Nonviolent Peacemaking, by Arthur Gish (Herald Press): Reports from Christian Peacemaker Teams worker in Hebron in the occupied West Bank.

Land of Revelation: A Reconciling Presence in Israel, by Roy Kreider (Herald Press): Memoir of long-term Mennonite Board of Mission worker in Israel.

Rethinking Holy Land: A Study in Salvation Geography, by Marlin Jeschke (Herald Press): Mennonite Bible professor examines biblical understandings of "holy land" and their relevance today.

Salt and Sign: Mennonite Central Committee in Palestine, 1949-1999, Alain Epp Weaver and Sonia Weaver (MCC): A brief history of MCC's work in Palestine.

Under Vine and Fig Tree: Biblical Theologies of Land and the Palestinian-Israeli Conflict, ed. Alain Epp Weaver (Cascadia): Study of biblical texts about land read in the light of current realities in Palestine-Israel.

Videos

Children of the Nakba (MCC): Accompany Palestinian refugees on trips back to their villages of origin and meet Israelis with the Zochrot Association who believe that refugee return is a vital part of durable peacebuilding.

The Dividing Wall (MCC): Shows the impact of the separation barrier on Palestinian communities and introduces viewers to Palestinians and Israelis working for a future of bridges intead of walls.

Walking the Path Jesus Walked (MCC): Tells the story of three Middle Eastern Christians, including Nora Carmi, a Palestinian Christian.

Web sites

Christian Peacmaker Teams: **www.cpt.org**
Eastern Mennonite Missions: **www.emm.org**
Mennonite Central Committee: **www.mcc.org**
Mennonite Church Canada Witness:
www.mennonitechurch.ca/programs/witness
Mennonite Mission Network:
www.mennonitemission.net
Nazareth Village: **www.nazarethvillage.com**

Online Resources: Essays and Newsletters

Christian Zionism and Peace in the Holy Land. MCC
Peace Office Newsletter, 35(3). July-September
2005: www.mcc.org/respub/pon/PON_2005-
07-01.pdf

Walling Off the Future for Palestinians and Israelis.
MCC Peace Office Newsletter, 34(3). July-
September 2004:
www.mcc.org/respub/pon/mcc_pon04_03.pdf

Country Profile: Occupied Palestinian Territories.
A Common Place. September/October 2004
(including the Hello publication for children):
www.mcc.org/acp/2004/sept_oct/acp_
septoct2004.pdf

**Peacebuilding in Palestine / Israel: A Discussion
Paper** meant to help facilitate a conversation in
communities back in North America about
stewardship, divestment, and economic justice,
online at www.mcc.org/papers/2005-
05_Peacebuilding_in_Palestine-Israel.pdf

Alain Epp Weaver, **Constantinianism, Zionism,
Diaspora: Toward a Theology of Exile and Return**
(MCC Occasional Paper #28, 2002):
www.mcc.org/respub/occasional/28.html

B. Other Resources for Further Learning
Books

Naim Ateek, **Justice and Only Justice**
(Maryknoll, NY: Orbis, 1986). A Palestinian
Christian theologian reads the Bible out of the
experience of occupation.

Gary Burge, **Whose Land? Whose Promise? What
Christians are Not Being Told about Israel and the
Palestinians** (Cleveland: The Pilgrim Press,
2003). An evangelical Christian New
Testament professor at Wheaton College reads
Scripture in light of the Palestinian-Israeli
conflict.

Marc Ellis, **Out of the Ashes** (London: Pluto
Press, 2002). Jewish-American scholar Marc
Ellis provides a searing analysis of the
Palestinian-Israeli conflict from a Jewish faith
perspective.

Amira Hass, **Drinking the Sea in Gaza** (New
York: Henry Holt, 1996). A leading Israeli
journalist chronicles life in Gaza during the
early 1990s.

Mitri Raheb, **I Am a Palestinian Christian**
(Minneapolis: Fortress Press, 1995). Pastor of
Christmas Lutheran Church in Bethlehem,

Raheb offers narrative and theological reflections on Palestine-Israel.

Tanya Reinhart, **Israel/Palestine: How to End the War of 1948** (New York: Seven Stories Press, 2002). A professor at Tel Aviv University presents a concise analysis of the roots of the Palestinian/Israeli conflict and discusses potential ways forward.

Raja Shehadeh, **When the Bulbul Stopped Singing** (London: Profile Books, 2003). Personal account of life in the West Bank town of Ramallah during the Israeli invasion of April 2002.

Ilan Pappé, **The History of Modern Palestine.** (Cambridge: Cambridge University Press, 2003). One of the leading Israeli historians presents a thorough discussion of the tumultuous events of the nineteenth and twentieth centuries.

Donald E. Wagner, **Anxious for Armageddon: A Call to Partnership for Middle Eastern and Western Christians** (Scottdale, Pa.: Herald Press, 1995). Discussion and critique of Christian Zionism by the president of Evangelicals for Middle East Understanding.

Munib Younan, **Witnessing for Peace: In Jerusalem and the World** (Minneapolis: Fortress Press, 2003). Poignant personal accounts and theological reflections from the Lutheran bishop of Jerusalem.

Web sites

Applied Research Institute-Jerusalem: **www.arij.org**. Maps and case studies on Israeli settlement activity in the Occupied Territories.

Badil Resource Center for Residency and Refugee Rights: **www.badil.org**. Leading Palestinian resource and advocacy center for researching and promoting durable solutions for Palestinian refugees.

Israeli Committee Against House Demolitions: **www.icahd.org/eng**. Critical Israeli perspectives on settlements and house demolitions.

Sabeel Ecumenical Liberation Theology Center: **www.sabeel.org**. News and reflections from Palestinian Christians.

Zochrot Association: **www.zochrot.org**. Web site for Israeli organization dedicated to "remembering the Nakba in Hebrew."

The Author

Sonia Weaver worked for 11 years with Mennonite Central Committee in the West Bank, the Gaza Strip, Jerusalem, and Jordan, most recently as co-representative for MCC's Palestine, Jordan, and Iraq programs. She is the co-author of *Salt and Sign: Mennonite Central Committee in Palestine, 1949-1999*. She is married to Alain Epp Weaver and has two children, Samuel and Katherine.